The Lord of Love

Alan Ames

....

In thanks to

A dear friend
Lesley Negley.

Contents

Preface 7
Introduction 9
Sacraments 10
Prayer 16
The Word of God 25
The Holy Trinity 27
Holy Spirit 29
Union in God 33
Adoration 34
Mysteries of God 34
Christmas 36
Divine Sacrifice 39
Salvation 52
Easter 53
Mother Mary 53
The Rosary 60
The Church 61
Religious Life 65
Obedience 70
Faith 71
Grace 74
Holiness 76
Souls 76
Heaven 78
Saints 80
Angels 83
Forgiveness 84

Mercy 87
Trust 88
Truth and Honesty . . 91
The Life of Jesus 97
Living in God 100
Imitating the Lord . . . 106
Working for God 111
Commitment 114
Perseverance 117
True Love 117
The Heart 128
Sharing 140
Kindness 143
Friendship 145
Creation 147
Mankind 150
Life 153
Death 166
Resurrection 170
The Gift of a Body . . . 170
Families 172
Marriage 175
Children of God 177
The Young 180
Choice 181
Happiness and Joy . . . 184
Confusion 189

Clarity 190
Truly Seeing 191
Wisdom 193
Denial 195
The Poor 195
Need 196
Suffering 197
Healing 200
Sacrifices 200
Hope 201
Blessings 202
Humility 203
Evil 204
Sin 207
Pride and Selfishness 209
Greed 212
Offering 212
Idolatry 214
Addictions 215
Violence and War 216
Peace 217
Jerusalem 219
God's Will 219
Justice 220
Law 220
Technology 221
Doctors 221
Judgement Day 222
The Reign of God 222

Preface

Today, sadly many seem to have forgotten that God is love and have a fear of God, but how can it be that we fear the one who loves us and only wants the best for each person? It should be that we embrace our loving Lord into our lives, not push Him away. It is by embracing Him that we humans can find what true love is and what it is to live in true love. It is by embracing Him that we can find the peace and security in our lives which brings us certainty and no fear. In the confusion of life today many wonder why life is so bad and wonder why it cannot be better. Well, life can be better by accepting Our Lord's love and by living in His love, for it is by doing this that people are open to His Divine Grace. His grace, which brings goodness and all that a person needs to live a better life. It is because so many deny Our Lord's love that they deny this wonderful grace and find their lives full of confusion and uncertainty. God from the beginning has told mankind He loves them and has continued to tell mankind of His love for all people. God from the beginning has said that if mankind lives in His way of love—loving Him above all else and loving each other, that life will be good. Mankind sadly has not listened and continues to suffer.

As you read these messages from The Lord of Love you will find that each one of them is loving and is there to lead people deep into the love of Christ, Our Lord. From the first word Our Lord Jesus spoke to me I knew He loved me and I knew I loved Him and with every word He continues to speak I know His love and I am strengthened in His love. In these words Our Lord makes it very clear that there is not one person He denies His love to, and that His desire is that all people will accept His love and accept the wonderful grace that comes with His love. My hope is that by sharing these beautiful words with others, as the Lord has asked me to, that those who read them will find in each word the same love that I have and be filled with the richness of God's love in a special way.

God love you,

Alan Ames

Introduction

As you read the messages, you will see some have scriptural references, while others have none. This is because in the beginning the Lord did not give me any references, but from December 1995 the Lord began to do so at various times. When I am given the references from Holy Scripture, it may be one or two lines, or only one or two words from a line. Sometimes two or three lines from different parts of Holy Scripture are combined to make the reference. The references at first were taken either from the Jerusalem or Douay-Rheims Bible, but later to avoid any confusion, my spiritual director and I decided to use only the New American Bible for references.

Sacraments

To come closer to Me, prayer and the Sacraments are the answer. Do not, in times of trouble, stop praying—increase your prayers, increase your taking of the Sacraments and find yourself deep in My heart.

Roses of love, the Sacraments.
Perfume of passion, the Sacraments.
Flowers of joy, the Sacraments.

Each sacrament is a rose with the sweetest perfume that I offer so that My children may become the flowers of love they were created to be.

Sacraments are sacred gifts.
Sacraments are sacred love.
Sacraments are sacred gifts given in love by God.

To draw on My love means to fill yourself with grace, to fill yourself with grace means to receive the Sacraments, to receive the Sacraments means you fill yourself with My love.

14/1/96

FILLED WITH MY love in My body.
Filled with My truth in My body.
Filled with My strength in My body.

There for all if they believe.
There for all if they repent.
There for all if they ask.

14/1/96

EATING AT MY table you receive the food of life.
Eating at My table you receive the filling of your soul.
Eating at My table you receive the gift of eternal love.

JOHN 6:35
I am the bread of life, he who comes to me will never be hungry, he who believes in me will never thirst.

....

24/1/96

In confession you cleanse
your heart and soul to
become pure in My love.

LUKE 11:4
*Forgive us our sins as we forgive everyone
that is indebted to us.*

4/2/96

LOOKING ON THE Holy Bread of communion you see Me. If you can look and understand this without doubts then you truly are close to Me.

JOHN 7:28
'Yes, you know me and you know where I came from.'

21/2/96

MY BODY, MY blood...My gift.

15/6/96

IN THE HOST, I am.
    In the Sacrament, I am.
    In the Mass, I am.

    I am there, believe it.

16/6/96

THE JOY IN the Mass is for all.
    The sacrifice,
    The offering,
    The love,
    The Mass.

2/9/96

SACRAMENTAL LIFE IS the true life,
    Sacramental life is a life of love,

    Sacramental life is the life God offers to all, the true life that brings true love.

ZECHARIAH 10:12 | *Their strength will be in Yahweh.*

13/11/96

THERE IS A path to walk that leads to heaven. It is a straight and true path. If you can walk it the rewards are great. If you stray, the suffering...terrible.

All are offered a guiding hand to help them stay on the path, all are offered a forgiving grace when they stray and all are offered the strength to walk it; the strength that is found in Me.

The guiding hand is the Word of God, the forgiving grace is through the Holy Spirit in the Sacrament of Confession and the strength is My body and blood found in the Eucharist.

....

2/2/97

Wrap My body around your soul.
Drench your spirit in My blood.
Every time you receive Me within in the Eucharist.

ISAIAH 34:21
There the Lord in majesty will be for us.

5/2/97

PRAYER, A GRACE, Love, a gift...
Sacraments, the gifts through which you will find many graces.

15/8/97

IN THE SACRAMENTS I await to fill you with goodness and joy. In the Sacraments I await to fill you with love and hope. In the Sacraments I await to fill you with Me.

MATTHEW 13:37 | *He who sows good seed is the son of man.*

19/8/97

WHEN YOU CONFESS your sins you show your soul to Me in a way that says, 'I am sorry, forgive me.'
When you confess your sins you show your soul to Me and I see the truth in your words. When you confess your sins you show your soul to Me so that I can, by the power of the Holy Spirit, heal you, purify you, and cleanse you of all that keeps you from Me.

Confession, so important, yet so forgotten. So needed, yet so rejected. So holy, yet so denied.
Come to confession and begin life anew in Me.

ACTS 10:43
Everyone who believes in him will receive forgiveness of sins through his name.

1/9/97

TO SEARCH YOUR heart and find your weaknesses, recognize them and then see in My love your heart is healed and your weaknesses forgiven.
That is a grace given in the Sacrament of confession, a grace that gives you the strength to overcome all weaknesses in your life.

MALACHI 1:5 | *Your own eyes shall see it.*

28/10/97

THE SACRAMENTS—STEPS TO heaven,
   The Sacraments—Strength of graces,
   The Sacraments—Sacred gifts.

PROVERBS 2:12 | *Saving you from the way of evil.*

....

1/11/97

Sacraments bring peace,
   Sacraments bring love,
   Sacraments bring you to Me.

PSALMS 141:1 | *I call to you.*

1/11/97

MY BODY AND blood.
   My love and forgiveness.
   My mercy and hope...

In the Sacraments.

LUKE 3:6 | *See the salvation of God.*

9/11/97

TO LOVE ME more, love the Sacraments.
   To love Me more, love prayer.
   To love Me more, love others.

20/11/97

SACRAMENTS—SACRED GIFTS.
Sacraments—sacred graces.
Sacraments—sacred gifts that fill you
with the grace of My love.

EZEKIEL 39:29 | *For I have poured out my spirit.*

Prayer

13/1/96

INTO MY HEART I place your prayers
and respond in love, only love.

Into My heart I place your petitions
and joyfully answer them.

Into My heart I place your very thoughts
and treasure them.

PSALMS 107:6
*Then they called to Yahweh in their trouble and he rescued
them from their sufferings.*

22/2/96

A GROUP OF CHILDREN before God in prayer
is a wonderful sight to behold.

Encourage prayer groups for they are dear to My heart.

3/3/96

IN PRAYER FIND peace,
  In prayer find comfort,
  In prayer find Me.
  Prayer, words with God,
  Prayer, words of God,
  Prayer, words for God.

  Through prayer strengthen your faith,
  Through prayer strengthen your heart,
  Through prayer strengthen your love.
  Prayer, such a special gift,
  Prayer, such a special time,
  Prayer, such a special hope.

  Praying, poetry from the heart,
  Praying, words that portray your love,
  Praying, communicating with love.
  Pray, pray, pray and find the true way.

4/3/96

TO PRAY FROM the heart is the best way to pray, for then
it is a prayer of love. The words are not so important as
the love in which they are given. Think of this love every
time you pray and see your prayers as a gift of love to
Me.

JOHN 8:31–32
If you make my word your home you will indeed be my
disciples, you will learn the truth and the truth will make
you free.

12/3/96

IN PRAYER FIND your strength,
In the Sacraments find your hope,
In love find Me.

15/3/96

WHEN THERE IS a difficult moment
come to Me in prayer.

MATTHEW 6:9 | *The Lord's prayer.*

24/3/96

TO ENCOURAGE PRAYER is to open hearts.
To encourage prayer is to save souls.
The encourage prayer is to please Me.

BARUCH 5:4 | *Through devotedness.*

8/4/96

A PRAYER OF HOPE,
a prayer of love,
a prayer of humility...

A prayer that is from your heart to God.

1/6/96

WHILE WALKING, PRAY,
While talking, pray,
While working, pray,
While playing, pray,
While resting, pray,
While relaxing, pray,
While breathing, pray,

Pray in everything you do.
Pray in every way you can.
Pray in love and see what you are.

ECCLESIASTICUS 47:89
In all his activities he gave thanks to the holy one,
the most high.

15/6/96

PRAY IN THANKS,
Pray in worship,
Pray in love...just pray.

30/6/96

SONGS OF PRAISE,
voices raised in love.
Sweet prayers.

15/7/96

WHEN YOU THINK of Me, you pray. When you send your love
to Me, you pray. When you wish you could spend time
with Me, you pray.

Every thought of love that you have for Me is a prayer I
receive in My heart.

26/7/96

PRAYER...WORDS OF LOVE,
Prayer...words of praise,
Prayer...words of the heart.

When you pray, pray in love, pray from your heart
and pray in praise of God's love for you.

PRAYER STRENGTHENS,
    Prayer brings peace,
    Prayer opens your heart to Me.

....

30/9/96

Pray in love, pray for love, pray with
love. This is how to pray, for in love
prayers are answered, with love gifts
are given and for love hearts are
opened.

14/12/96

IN PRAYER FIND peace,
    In prayer find the answers,
    In prayer find Me.

I am the answer to all your prayers
and I am the bringer of peace.

15/12/96

WHEN YOU REACH out to Me in love I am there to take your
hand and answer your prayers.

ECCLESIASTICUS 15:6
He will find happiness and a crown of joy.

18/1/97

PRAYERS FOR PEACE, prayers for love, prayers for hope...
Prayers bring peace to those who pray in love and hope
in Me.

PHILEMON: 61
Pray that this faith will give rise to a sense of fellowship that
will show you all the good things we are able to do for Christ.

20/1/97

THE TIME YOU spend in prayer strengthens
your soul and softens your heart.

ISAIAH 22:25
And the whole load hanging on it will be shattered.

18/3/97

PRAYER STRENGTHENS, PRAYER fills, prayer opens, when
you pray it opens your heart to be filled and strengthened
in My love.

20/4/97

LITTLE GIFTS OF love...prayers.
Little graces of God...prayers.

Little gifts that can bring many graces
if you open your heart in prayer.

20/4/97

AS YOU PRAY, pray for the strength to pray more.
As you pray, pray for the strength to pray from your
heart.
As you pray, pray for the strength to pray in humility.

22/5/97

IN YOUR PRAYERS see the love you offer Me.
In your prayers see the love I return to you.
In your prayers see the love of God in you from Me.

ACTS 6:4 | *Devote ourselves to prayer.*

6/6/97

YOUR WORRYING CHANGES nothing but your prayers do.

TOBIT 13:6 | *With all your heart and all your soul.*

18/6/97

PRAYER STRENGTHENS. PRAYER brings you closer to Me.
Prayer is always answered when it is for good. Pray!

SIRACH 36:16
*He who serves God willingly is heard; his petition reaches
the heavens.*

24/6/97

ALL PRAYERS OF love are God-inspired.

29/6/97

PRAYERS, SACRAMENTS AND love lead you to Me. Hope, faith
and charity are found in Me. Trust, belief and generosity
bring you nearer to Me.
When you pray, if you are generous in your offerings for
others, you will find My charity waiting to answer your
hopes in Me.
When you receive the Sacraments if you have faith and believe in Me your trust will strengthen the love in your heart
and fill you with the graces to bring you nearer to Me.

When you love the Sacraments and desire to pray you will find yourself led closer and closer to me then your hopes will be fulfilled in eternity.

ECCLESIASTICUS 7:9–10
Do not be impatient in prayer; do not be impatient to give alms.

1/7/97

PRAY FOR THOSE who are under the yoke of sin.
  Pray for their burden to be lifted.
  Pray for those who oppress as well as those they oppress.

ECCLESIASTICUS 40:1
Much hardship has been made for every man,
a heavy yoke lies on the sons of Adam.

....

6/7/97

Prayers can strengthen hearts,
      heal souls and cure bodies,
      all it takes is faith and trust.

JONAH 2:3
I called to the Lord and he answered me.

7/8/97

A PRAYER OF THANKS is always welcome.
  A prayer of thanks is a prayer of recognition.
  A prayer of thanks is a sign of humble acceptance of God's mercy.

TO SEEK ETERNITY, pray,
    To seek heaven, pray,
    To seek God, pray.

    Prayer will lead you to Me and in Me you will find
    eternal joy awaiting in heaven.

    ZECHERIAH 3:6
    If you walk in my ways and heed my charge.

PRAYERS ARE ANSWERED; it is just
    that not everyone sees this nor believes it.

    PSALMS 37:4
    Find your delight in the Lord who will give you your heart's
    desire.

UNITED IN PRAYER your hearts are united in love.
    United in prayer your voices are united in praise.
    United in prayer your souls are united in Me.

PRAYERS OF LOVE, open hearts.
    Prayers of love, open souls.
    Prayers of love, open the gates of heaven.

A PRAYER OF THANKS is a prayer of grace and a prayer of
    grace should be said with thanks.

11/10/97

PRAYERFUL PEOPLE ARE the people who help save the lost souls who do not pray. Prayerful people are the people who help spread God's love by the giving and offering of their prayers. Prayerful people are the people who help strengthen the Church by their commitment to God. Special people who have special rewards awaiting them in the next life.

JEREMIAH 4:2 | *And glory in him.*

19/11/97

PRAYER BRINGS YOUR focus on Me.
Prayer brings your heart to Mine.
Prayer brings your soul the strength
it needs from My love.

MATTHEW 7:7 | *Seek and you will find.*

The Word of God

4/12/95

ALONG THE ROAD of life are many diversions that are there to lead you away from the path of love. Each of these diversions is put there as a trap to ensnare you but often they do not seem like that. Often they look appealing, welcoming and safe. Often they appear as reasonable, as a proper choice to make. It is so hard at times to discover what is truth and what is deceit.

It is no wonder many falter and take the wrong path. Sometimes they falter because they are weak and sometimes because they did not listen to the directions given to them so they would stay on the path of life. The map to follow is laid out before all, they only have to read it and follow it.

If they do this they will find the strength they need to carry on and the directions they need to follow. They are found in the Holy Scriptures, in the Word of God. They are so plain to see, so easy to understand but to many so hard to follow.

31/3/96

THE BOOK OF Holy Scripture is the Word of God
and the Word of God is the truth.

JOHN 8:47 | *A child of God listens to the words of God.*

29/11/96

IN HOLY SCRIPTURE find the truth of life and the life of truth. I am the truth and I am life.

JOHN 3:33 | *Anyone who believes in the Son has eternal life.*

7/1/97

FROM THE WORD of God comes life.
From the Word of God comes creation.
From the Word of God comes love.

I am the Word.

29/4/97

IN HOLY SCRIPTURE you find the truth if you look with an open heart and mind; open to God and closed to self.

MATTHEW 5:21 | *How it was said to our ancestors.*

19/5/97

A WORD OF LOVE is always welcome, A word of comfort often sought, A word of hope often needed.

I am the Word and I am the love that brings comfort and hope to those in need when they welcome Me into their lives.

The Holy Trinity

12/2/96

THE RESURRECTION SAYS to mankind death is not the end but the beginning. The ascension says to mankind after death heaven awaits those who believe. The descent of the Holy Spirit says to mankind God has so many gifts to give them if they trust.
When I arose from the dead I showed I am God. When I ascended to heaven I showed I am one with the Father. When the Holy Spirit descended He showed that He is one with Me and My Father.

The Holy Trinity of God each separate yet each the same.

17/2/96

THE FATHER AND the Son with the Spirit, One.

> MATTHEW 22:32
> *I am the God of Abraham, the God of Isaac and the God of*
> *Jacob.*

11/3/96

THE SPIRIT FILLS you when you receive My body for I and the Spirit are one. The Father touches you when you receive My body for I and the Father are one.

In union with Me you are filled with the Holy Trinity in love and in peace.

28/9/96

PRAISE THE FATHER,
Glorify the Spirit
and in Me love God.

8/3/97

THE TRINITY OF God, the triangle of love.
The trinity of God, the one true love.
The trinity of God, the beginning and
the end of all love.

The love of God, the one true love
that exists forever in the trinity of love.

8/12/97

IN THIS TIME of Advent it is good to reflect upon the events that occurred leading up to My birth. It is good to look at them and see the hand of My Father and the power of

the Holy Spirit fulfilling the prophecies of old and bringing to mankind a new understanding of God in the Holy
Trinity.
There is much to reflect on and much to learn from if you
look with a heart of faith and eyes of hope.

LUKE 8:50 | *Just have faith.*

Holy Spirit

27/1/96

THE FIRE OF love, My Holy Spirit.
   The wind of God, My Holy Spirit.
   The gift of God's love, My Holy Spirit.

God...the Holy Spirit.

WISDOM 1:6 | *Wisdom is a spirit, a friend to man.*

17/2/96

THE HOLY SPIRIT lifts the hearts of mankind to God.
   The Holy Spirit opens the hearts of mankind to God
   The Holy Spirit fills the hearts of mankind with God.

JOHN 12:32
*And when I am lifted up from the earth, I shall draw all men
unto myself.*

12/4/96

Grace-filled are those that the Holy
Spirit touches; they only need to
recognize this and accept it to reach
their full potential in God.

1/5/96

FRESHNESS OF THE Spirit comes with prayer,
strength of the Spirit comes in the Sacraments,
power of the Spirit comes in faith.

When you pray, believe and feel The Spirit flow through
you in the Sacraments you receive.

EXODUS 4:21
*You will perform all the miraculous signs that I have empow-
ered you to do.*

5/5/96

JUST AS THE wind blows unseen by man so My Spirit goes
around the world. As you see the trees bend when the
wind touches them so you see the hearts of men change
as the Holy Spirit touches them.

26/5/96

MY SPIRIT GIVES life, life in God.
My Spirit brings hope, hope in God.
My Spirit offers gifts, gifts in God.

Through My Spirit find the life that brings
hope to all as a gift from the Father.

26/5/96

WATCHING A WATERFALL one day a man wondered at the
power of the water, a power that originated from a little
spring in the mountains to become such a great force.
So it is with the gifts of the Holy Spirit. At first they seem
so small but as they flow and are allowed to grow in faith
the gifts become a great force for goodness.

27/5/96

AS A BIRD flies in the sky it often floats on the wind. So it
must be for those who are gifted by God; they must float
in the will of God through the Holy Spirit. It is when you
trust that the Spirit of God will supply all that is needed
to keep you on the path to heaven, just as the bird trusts
in the wind to keep it aloft, you will find the gifts of God
grow in you.

1/6/96

THE DOVE OF peace is within the hearts of those who receive
My body. They only have to set Him free to be filled with
My love.

15/6/96

THE HOLY SPIRIT...
So strong in moving hearts.
So strong in opening doors.
So strong in love.

9/4/97

IN THE HOLY Spirit find the graces and gifts you need.
In the Holy Spirit find Me.

18/5/97 (Pentecost)

WHEN MY HOLY Spirit came upon the Apostles He was showing mankind that God's Spirit is there for all.

When the Apostles spoke in different tongues the Holy
Spirit was saying whatever language you speak, whatever
race you are, I am here for you if you want Me.

When the Apostles went forth and spread the good news
by the power of the Holy Spirit mankind was being shown
that the power of God is there for all if they humbly accept God's will.

What My Holy Spirit showed the world is that with the
love of God in your life God will fill you with His gifts and
graces so that you can bring the Spirit of God to others
and then find your eternal rest in heaven.

ACTS 10:44–48 | *Baptism of the first pagans.*

2/7/97

When you look at the clouds in the
sky drifting across the heavens
guided by the wind, think of how
your soul can be guided by the wind
of the Holy Spirit, if you do not resist
and accept the direction the Spirit of
God wishes to take you.

ECCLESIASTICUS 6:37
He will strengthen your mind and the wis-
dom you desire will be granted.

15/7/97

TO PREPARE FOR confession, open your heart to the Holy
Spirit and ask for His guidance. With an empty mind and
an open heart He will reveal to you what is needed to confess.

ZECHERIAH 4:4 | *What are these things my Lord.*

Union in God

24/7/96

SPIRITUAL UNION, AN union of love,
 Spiritual union, an union of souls,
 Spiritual union, an union of God and man.

29/7/97

UNITED FOREVER IN love, those who love Me.
 United forever in love, those who receive Me within.
 United forever in love, those who believe in My presence.

21/9/97

REFRESH YOURSELF IN Me.
 Refresh yourself through Me.
 Refresh yourself with Me.
 United in the Eucharist.

LUKE 1:53 | *The hungry he has filled with good things.*

Adoration

8/4/96

COME AND SIT with Me.
> Come and be with Me.
> Come and love Me.

9/12/97

TIME ALONE WITH Me is time well spent, for in these moments of silence My love for you can become much clearer.

PHILIPPIANS 1:16 | *Aware that I am here.*

Mysteries of God

14/4/96

I AM INCOMPREHENSIBLE TO many. Many cannot understand how I can love them, how I can continue to love them even when they make the mistakes of sin.

My love can never be understood on earth but in heaven you can come to see the completeness of My love.

ECCLESIASTICUS 43:20
The eyes marvel at the beauty of its whiteness.

2/8/96

I AM ONE WITH the Father and the Spirit. There is the mystery of God that can never be understood by man.

Life, created from God to return to God—a mystery that confuses so many. Love, created of God for God is love—a mystery that many reject. Eternity, God's gift awaiting those who believe—a mystery of faith that many ignore.

To ignore or reject anything that confuses you or you cannot understand is a mistake. Let your faith show you the truth and let the truth lead you to eternal life in heaven.

I am the truth.

MALACHI 3:7 | *Return to me and I will return to you.*

18/11/96

IN THE BEGINNING I was, now I am, forever I will be. This does not change because mankind believes or not, it just is!

19/12/96

IN THE BEGINNING was God
and in the beginning with the Father, I am.

ECCLESIASTICUS 42:17
For the universe to stand firm in his glory.

21/9/97

FOREVER I AM loving.
Forever I am forgiving.
Forever I am.

EPHESIANS 5:5 | *In the kingdom of Christ and of God.*

Christmas

25/12/95

WHEN I CAME to earth I came to free mankind. I came to show how much God loves mankind. I came as God's gift of Himself to man.

Now I ask for My children to see the truth in the gift of God, the gift of freedom and accept it so that they may live in God's love forever.

25/12/95

ON THIS DAY God came to earth through His beloved daughter, My Mother, Mary. When I came, I came to free sinners, to defeat evil and this began with My first breath and finished with My last.

My life on earth, a gift from the beginning to the end.
My life on earth, a sacrifice that was the beginning
of the end of evil.
My life on earth, a union of man and God.
My life on earth, a signpost on how to live.
My life on earth, a sharing of God's mercy.
My life on earth, a treasure for mankind.
My life on earth, the greatest act of love.

25/12/95

AS I LAY in the manger looking up into My Mother's eyes, I looked into her soul and only saw love. As she gently smiled at Me, My heart was filled with her love and I returned My love to fill her heart. As she reached down to pick Me up I could feel the gentleness in her hands, I could smell the perfume of her love and I could see the warmth of her soul.

Mary, My Mother, waits to embrace all her children and give them her love so that as Mary's heart was, theirs too could be filled with My love.

25/12/95

THE SMELL OF the hay,
        The sound of the animals,
        The joy of My Mother and Joseph,
        The Birth of God.

        The star in the sky,
        The angels singing,
        The shepherds visiting,
        The Birth of God.

        The Baby Jesus,
        The Son of God,
        The Child of heaven,
        The Birth of God.

25/12/95

FROM HEAVEN CAME God to bring His children home.
From heaven came God to forgive sin.

From heaven came God to open His heart and show how much He loved mankind.

25/12/95

THE JOY THAT fills the heavens today...
   The joy of the birthday of God.

   The happiness that fills the heart of God...
   The happiness of saving souls.

   The glory that fills the air...
   The glory of God's love.

25/12/96

THE JOY THAT fills hearts on My birthday
   should fill hearts every day.

   PSALMS 85:12 | *Yahweh himself bestows happiness.*

25/12/96

TO CELEBRATE MY birthday with joy in your heart
   brings the true meaning of Christmas to life.

25/12/96

AS MY MOTHER wrapped her arms around Me I could feel the warmth of her love touching My heart. As each breath she took gently touched My skin I could feel the love of God's chosen daughter embrace My soul. As each smile she made reached My eyes I could feel the joy of her complete abandonment to God's will surround My body. Surrounded by love, embraced by love and touched by love, I lay at peace in My mother's arms.

   BARUCH 4:36 | *See the joy that is coming to you from God.*

Divine Sacrifice

12/12/95

I SUFFERED FOR MY family on earth. I offered Myself to the
Father as the sacrifice that forgives mankind's sins. I re-
deemed My children so that they could be happy in God's
love forever.

How I suffer each time one of My children refuses what I
offer and denies the redemption that is his by the sacrifice of My body for his forgiveness.

12/12/95

THE PAIN AS I hung on the cross was so deep I could feel it
within My soul. It does not compare however, with the
pain I feel each time a soul is lost. That pain is the deep-
est sorrow and anguish I feel. Imagine then how painful it is with so many souls lost, with so many denying
God.

13/12/95

AS THE BLOOD ran down My face and fell onto the ground
I gave Myself for the world as a sacrifice to forgive mankind's sins.

As the wounds in My body tore on the nails I cried to the
Father to forgive mankind's sins.

As I rose from the dead I showed mankind's sins had been
forgiven and if mankind accepted this forgiveness eternal life with God was theirs.

26/12/95

EVERY DAY REMEMBER My sacrifice, remember what I gave for you and all My children. Remember and accept what I offered with My sacrifice; God's love and God's mercy.

29/12/95

As I hang on the cross with My heart opened to the world I shower all of mankind with My forgiving love, My love which is offered to strengthen, to fill and to lift souls to God. They only have to accept it for this to happen.

3/1/96

AS I LOOKED upon My family on earth while I hung on the cross I was aware of all the sins that have been and would be committed.

Through all this I could still see the love that was there and which was often hidden. I knew sin would not stop on the day I died but it was defeated. How can this be? Surely if something is defeated it should stop! The defeat of sin was complete and sin will stop, it is only that mankind prolongs the final day of sin. Once mankind accepts evil is defeated it will stop, once mankind brings into the open its true self, the self of love, sin will stop.

The evil one cannot accept his defeat and so he encourages mankind to allow sin to grow as he believes by this he can overcome the defeat I inflicted upon him by My sacrifice on the cross.

He does not understand he has lost and no matter how much more mankind sins he can never win. Mankind must come to understand the only thing left before the final day is how many souls will be lost and how many will be saved. All can be saved if all want to be.

Make the right decisions and end the agony on earth before it is the final day.

8/1/96

THE PAIN I felt on the cross was the pain of all mankind's sins. The sorrow I carried on My heart was the sorrow of all mankind's wrongs. The truth I showed with My sacrifice is the truth of God's merciful forgiveness which is there for all mankind.

8/1/96

DRIPPING WITH BLOOD, the crown that pierced My head. Dripping with blood, the nails that pierced My hands and feet. Dripping with blood, the spear that pierced by body.

Each wound flooded the world with My precious blood. Each wound opened the doorway to heaven. Each wound brought forgiveness.

The wounds, the blood and the forgiveness—one in the redemption of mankind.

14/1/96

AS I HUNG on the cross in pain I looked into the hearts of those around Me. I could see hate, anger, love, joy, sadness, pity, confusion and torment.

I saw the hate the Pharisees had for a blasphemer. I saw the anger the soldiers had for a troublemaker.

I saw the love My Mother has for Me. I saw the joy of that love. I saw the sadness in her heart for Me, her Son, being treated so. I saw the pity of those who gazed upon My broken body. I saw the confusion of My followers who wondered why this had to happen.

Then I saw the torment of the evil one as he saw his defeat and the salvation of mankind.

JOHN 19:30 | *It is accomplished.*

1/2/96

It hurts when love is denied.
        It hurts when truth is opposed.
        It hurts when hope is ignored.

        It hurt on the cross.

5/2/96

As I BLED on the cross each drop of blood I shed was enough to soften the hearts of all the sinners in the world, if only they would accept it.

As I cried to the Father to forgive them, the forgiveness asked was for all mankind if only they would accept it.

As I drew My last breath it was a breath I share with all mankind, a breath to cleanse mans' souls if only they would accept it.

As I look down from heaven I offer My love, My forgiveness and My saving grace to all mankind if only they will accept it.

JOHN 19:37 | *They will look upon the one they have pierced.*

JOHN 12:44 | *Whoever believes in me.*

JOHN 12:36 | *Will become sons of light.*

11/2/96

THE BLOOD THAT dripped from the cross was an offering, an offering to the Father for the forgiveness of mankind. It was also an offering to mankind, an offering of God's love, an offering of forgiveness and an offering of hope. The Father accepted willingly My offering. Will mankind?

COLOSSIANS 1:13–14
Because that is what he has done: He has taken us out of the power of darkness and created a place for us in the kingdom of the Son that he loves, and in him we gain our freedom, the forgiveness of our sins.

12/2/96

AS MY LIFE on earth ends, eternal life is offered to all. As My last breath leaves My body, My love is offered to all. As I cry to the Father with My final words on earth, forgiveness is offered to all.
The end of My life is a new beginning offered to mankind, a new life and a new hope. I offer it to all in love and only ask for love in return.

5/3/96

THE PAIN OF love,
>The pain of the cross,
>The pain of rejection.

>The joy of love,
>The joy of the cross,
>The joy of redemption.

>The sacrifice of love,
>The sacrifice of the cross,
>The sacrifice of the Saviour...

>A divine mercy for mankind.

....

12/3/96

In agony I forgave.
>In hope I offer.
>In love I wait.

17/3/96

A CROSS OF LOVE stood on the hill at Calvary. A cross of forgiveness was raised on the hill at Calvary. A cross of hope stands throughout eternity offering forgiveness and love to all.

Each person will need to climb their own Calvary to find the truth awaiting them in My sacrifice.

31/3/96

TO SUFFER FOR love.
    To give for peace.
    To offer for hope.

On the cross I offered, I gave, and I suffered for man.

....

2/4/96

The joy, the pain,
    Again and again.

        The love, the hate,
        The door to mankind's fate.

        The truth, the lies,
        One to follow, the other to despise.

        God's Son, evil defeated,
        Accept the gift and see sin eliminated.

5/4/96

THE PAIN ON the cross is the pain of man's sins.
    Lift the sin and lift the pain.

12/4/96

THE CROSS IS the hope.
    The cross is the future.
    The cross is the way.

13/5/96

THE PAIN I carried on the cross was all of mankind's pain. The sin I carried on the cross was all of mankind's sin. The forgiveness I offer on the cross is for all mankind, if only they ask.

MATTHEW 14:32
'Man of little faith,' he said, 'Why did you doubt?'

2/6/96

AN OFFER OF love,
An offer of peace,
An offer of truth...

My offering on the cross.

....

13/6/96

I hung alone on the cross in body, but in Spirit many were with Me. All those who love Me were there with Me and their prayers brought joy to My heart in My passion.

11/7/96

IN AGONY I hung on the cross looking upon My lost children. In agony I hung on the cross reaching out to My lost children. In agony I hung on the cross seeing all the sins mankind had done and would do.

I still reach out and offer My forgiveness, My guiding hand and I still feel the pain every time someone turns away and embraces sin.

17/8/96

A VISION OF THE cross,
> A vision of the love,
> A vision of the sacrifice.

The cross showed how much I love mankind and the sacrifice how much I was prepared to give to save them.

ECCLESIASTICUS 48:10 | *To restore the tribes of Jacob.*

15/9/96

IN MY BLOOD, forgiveness.
> In My blood, mercy.
> In My blood, love.

1/10/96

IN MY DEATH find life,
> In My death find forgiveness,
> In My death find hope,

In My death is the forgiveness many hope will bring them to eternal life. In My death is the hope that My forgiveness will bring an eternity in love. In My death is the lifeline for all those who seek it, the lifeline to heaven.

In My death is the truth of God's love.

25/11/96

ON THE CROSS I showed My love for mankind when I showed how much I was prepared to sacrifice to save My family on earth from eternal damnation.

When I turned to the sinner on the cross beside Me and forgave him his sins I showed mankind that even at the moment of death I will forgive, if it is asked for and if the asking is truly from the heart.

I showed mankind with My words, 'Forgive them Father for they know not what they do,' that no matter how mankind could abuse Me or no matter that they rejected My love, no matter they closed their eyes to the truth, My love and forgiveness was strong enough to overcome all this and that My love was offered to all.

Mankind needs to look to the cross and open their eyes to what I offered them and why, then come to Me and ask and I will answer.

25/3/97

AS I HUNG on the cross with pain racking My body I also was filled with the forgiving love of the Father which I offered to My family on earth. The love of the Father hung on the cross united in My suffering love and the healing love of the Spirit joined Me to make the Trinity of love reaching out from the cross offering mankind the way home.

On the cross God showed the depth of His love for mankind, now mankind needs to show the depth of its love for God.

To show this love My family on earth must pray for the opening of hearts to My sacrifice. To show this love, they must persevere even when all seems lost. To show this love they must continue to trust in Me that I will care for them. To show this love they must walk their lives without running from the crosses I may ask them to carry. To show this love they must share the love of God with others. To show this love they must not be afraid or worried about what may happen in the future. To show this love they must trust in God that whatever happens is in God's plan and therefore can only be for the best.

When My family on earth can do this the family will grow and will bring many lost children home.

28/3/97

IN THE GARDEN I overcame My human self and revealed My divinity. In the Garden I overcame My struggle within and revealed My obedience to My Father. In the Garden I overcame My weakness and revealed the strength of God's love.

Look to the Garden and learn how to be obedient, how to be strong in times of weakness and how to show your love of God.

ISAIAH 5:16
The Holy God will display his holiness by his integrity.

28/3/97 (Good Friday)

ALONE AS I hung on the cross I reached out and offered all of mankind the opportunity to join Me, to unite with Me, not only in the suffering but in the joy to come in the new life in heaven. When this offer is accepted many will come to find that the rewards far outweigh the suffering and that the rewards are eternal whereas the suffering came to an end.

18/6/97

THE PRECIOUS BLOOD that flowed from My heart on the cross is a river of forgiveness and a fountain of love for the world, a river that never stops flowing.

DANIEL 3:39
But with contrite heart and humble spirit let us be received.

6/7/97

THE BLOOD I shed on the cross was the blood of forgiveness which washed all sin away in those who bathe in My love and accept My forgiveness.

MATTHEW 5:7 | *For they will be shown mercy.*

11/8/97

MY HEART, MY soul, My spirit—all reaching out from the cross in love to mankind, love that says, 'I forgive you and I long for you to be with Me.' Love that says in your heart My love will brighten your soul and lift your spirit to heaven when you accept Me within and welcome Me there.

The cross, the true sign of love for mankind.
The cross, the true offer of forgiveness.
The cross, the only way of salvation.

MATTHEW 21:5 | *Behold your king,*

MATTHEW 4:32 | *As God has forgiven you in Christ.*

26/8/97

THE SACRIFICE OF the lamb, so often forgotten, but still with My sacrifice evil was defeated and those who seek it were forgiven, this does not change just because some choose to ignore it.

LAMENTATIONS 3:22
The favours of the lord are not exhausted his mercies are not spent.

13/9/97

THE PRECIOUS BLOOD I spilled on the cross is precious to everyone who seeks refuge in it. The precious blood I spilled on the cross is precious to the whole of creation. The precious blood I spilled on the cross is precious because it is the blood of love and of forgiveness.

In My precious blood I offer a refuge to all and I offer My forgiving love as a sign to the whole of creation of the mercy of God.

PSALMS 41:2 | *The Lord delivers them.*

15/10/97

A SIGN OF LOVE—THE cross.
A sign of love—My suffering.
A sign of love—My forgiveness.

27/10/97

AS I LOOKED down from the cross and saw each person I saw all the sins they had committed, all the wrongs they did but I also saw all the Sacraments they received, all the prayers they said and all the good they did.

The good shone brightly through the dark showing that many would accept My sacrifice but the dark showed that some, no matter what, would refuse to believe.

As I looked I was filled with sorrow from the sin, the evil and the disbelief but I was also filled with joy from the light of goodness shining brightly.

As I looked I reached out through eternity offering the hope that would save many and offering salvation to all.

SIRACH 2:7 | *Turn not away lest you fall.*

Salvation

7/4/96

A LOST HEART CAN be found.
　　A lost soul can be saved.
　　A lost spirit can be filled...

　　All by the love of God.

31/3/97

MAKE PEACE YOUR catch-cry,
　　make hope your words,
　　make salvation your message.

ECCLESIASTICUS 37:26
The fruits of his understanding are certain.

27/6/97

THE PAIN ENDURED for love is a pain worthwhile. The pain endured for salvation is the pain of grace. The pain endured for mankind is the pain of forgiveness.

All I endured, I endured for love, so that mankind could be forgiven and offered salvation. The grace offered from the cross is the grace of love that mankind should see as worthwhile if he truly wants to be saved.

AMOS 5:14
And that Yahweh, God of Sabaoth may really be with you.

Easter

....

30/3/97

Easter, a time of graces if people
        only seek them.
        Easter, a time of love if people
        only recognize it.
        Easter, a time of hope if people only
        look in expectation.

Mother Mary

8/12/95

TWO HEARTS FULL of love,
>One heart of God above,
>One heart a sweet daughter,
>Whose love is full of laughter.

>United in love,
>Joined by the dove,
>Mother and Son,
>Two hearts that become one.

24/1/96

MY MOTHER MARY, a pure love, a pure soul and a pure heart. My mother Mary, a pure love of God and mankind. A pure soul with no sin. A pure heart longing to share the rewards of God with all.

My mother Mary, your mother and all of mankind's mother.

MATTHEW 1:23
Behold a virgin shall be with child and shall bring forth a son and they shall call his name Emmanuel, which being interpreted is, God with us.

MATTHEW 8:10
Verily I say unto you I have not found so great faith.

4/3/96

MY **MOTHER, THE** mother for all,
    My mother, the help for all,
    My mother, the love for all.

    My mother, mankind's mother,
    My mother, mankind's help,
    My mother, mankind's love.

    My mother's love, there for all mankind,
    My mother's help, offered to all mankind,
    My mother's heart, opened to all mankind.

    Like a true mother she loves all her children and only
    wants to help them find the heart of God.

21/3/96

TO **LOVE MY** mother is to love your mother for on the cross I
    gave all of mankind My mother as theirs.
    To love My mother is to accept a gift of God, the gift of a
    mother's love that comes from the Father and is offered
    to all.
    To love My mother is to appreciate the sacrifice mother
    gave for all of mankind, the sacrifice of love through her
    Son, Jesus.

ECCLESIASTICUS 6:27
She will reveal herself to you.

ECCLESIASTICUS 6:29
And she will take the form of joy for you.

29/3/96

Mother of all,
Mother of Mine.

Mother of yours,
Mother of Mine.

Mother of God,
Mother of Mine.

8/4/96

AS QUEEN OF heaven mother is Queen of earth.
As Queen of heaven mother is Queen of souls.
As Queen of heaven mother is Queen of love.

Mother, who wants to love all the souls on earth and bring them to heaven.

REVELATIONS 12:1
Now a great sign appeared in heaven: A woman, adorned with the sun, standing on the moon, and twelve stars on her head for a crown.

12/4/96

MOTHER SHOWS LOVE in her humility.

3/5/96

IN MY MOTHER'S heart
you find the love of all mothers,
for she is mother of all.

9/7/96

GOOD PEOPLE CAN easily be confused to become fanatical
believers of false truths. My mother was My mother and
in a physical way mother to no other. In a spiritual way
she is mother to all. Through the taking of a human body
I became a brother to all and all became My brothers and
sisters. During My time on earth My family were not only
My cousins, My uncles, My aunts, but all who lived.
The words written of My brothers and sisters talk of those
people who were part of My extended and distant family,
for all those in a family were called brothers and sisters.
There is but the truth and that is My mother Mary is immaculate, I was conceived by the Holy Spirit. My mother
bore no other child and I am One with the Father and the
Holy Spirit. Any other truth is a deception, any other in-
terpretation of Holy Scripture is wrong. Anything else is
sent to confuse good people and to take them away from
Me.

29/11/96

THROUGH THE LOVE of My mother many find Me.
Through the love of My mother many find life.
Through the love of My mother many find peace.

The love of My mother, God's gift to mankind.
The love of My mother, God's love in mankind.
The love of My Mother, God's grace for mankind.

JEREMIAH 34:13
*Yahweh, the God of Israel says this: I made a covenant with
your ancestors.*

11/2/97

IMMACULATE MARY, MY mother,
   Immaculate Mary, your mother,
   Immaculate Mary, mother to all.

2 CHRONICLES 26:12 | *It was God's doing.*

30/5/97

IN MY MOTHER'S arms all can find Me.

15/8/97

WITH THE ASSUMPTION of My mother I confirmed to the world that she was free from sin, for if she had a sin in her being, her assumption would have been impossible.
With the assumption of My mother I said to mankind how special and how pure she was and that mankind should praise and thank her in an unique way for her life of love.
With the assumption of My mother I showed mankind that My mother waits in heaven to help her children on earth join her in the eternal bliss that is heaven.
Mary, assumed to heaven by God, deserves the respect and veneration of mankind. If this is not given it is mankind's loss and Mary's sorrow.

HOSEA 4:4 | *Let no one protest let no one complain.*

15/9/97

THE SORROWFUL HEART of My mother will become the joyful heart of Mary when sin is defeated and love reigns in all hearts.

PSALMS 33:5 | *And fills the earth with goodness.*

22/10/97

MY MOTHER HAS been appearing and speaking to many people throughout history and today it continues. The message she brings is the message of repentance, of love and of hope.

Mother's message is the message of conversion of hearts and souls. Mother's message is the message that calls all to holiness. Mother's message is the message that calls all to Me as mother's message is My message.

ACTS 10:17 | *The meaning of the vision.*

....

22/10/97

To find Me look to My mother who will
lead you to the Sacraments where I am.

WISDOM 24:2 | *In the presence of his hosts.*

4/12/97

THE IMMACULATE HEART of My mother is united in My heart to bring My love to the world. The immaculate heart of My mother is one with Me in her desire to lead many home to heaven. The immaculate heart of My mother is submissive to My will in all things and wants the hearts of her children on earth to be the same.

1 TIMOTHY 2:2
That we may lead a quiet and tranquil life in all devotion and dignity.

The Rosary

4/3/96

THE ROSARY, A prayer of love. The Rosary, a meditation of love. The Rosary, a gift of love. The Rosary, a special prayer given as a gift of love through My mother.
The Rosary, a meditation on My life which becomes a gift of love through My mother. The Rosary, a gift of love that through meditating on My life becomes a prayer of true love.

8/4/96

THE ROSARY, A meditation on My life.
The Rosary, prayer with My mother to Me.
The Rosary, a special gift I treasure.

JOHN 4:10 | *If you only knew what God is offering.*

9/7/96

A ROSARY OF LOVE is a powerful petition through My mother to God. A Rosary of love is a powerful gift that is given to help overcome evil. A Rosary of love comes from God through My Mother as a gift that will be listened to and answered in love.

My mother's Rosary, a joyful gift from God to His children.

The Church

5/7/96

UNITY IN THE Church is so important for My will to be expressed through it. Unity amongst the churches is so important in the defeat of evil; for united in My love My Church is strong. Unity under My chosen vessel is so important because it shows the acceptance of My will and the humility of those who love Me.

My chosen one was Peter and is all those who take the keys Peter passed on.

LAMENTATIONS 39:40–41
Let us examine our path, let us ponder it and return to Yahweh. Let us stretch out our hearts and hands to God in heaven.

6/7/96

MY HOUSE IS open to all but who comes?
My heart is open to all but who wants?
My love is there for all but who cares?

Come to My house and visit Me with an open heart and I will fill you with My love.

16/8/96

UNITY WITHIN THE Church is essential, for without unity how can My message of love be spread. It is the duty of My servants to be united in humble love under My chosen shepherd, the Pope. Disobedience to this shows a disregard for My will and shows the world a confused message. My servants must be just that, humble servants of God who follow God's will, not their own.

PSALMS 104:31
Glory to Yahweh forever, may Yahweh find joy in what he creates.

20/1/97

THE CATHOLIC CHURCH...MY body.
 The Catholic Church...My living gift.
 The Catholic Church...My bride.

....

20/1/97

The Pope, the Church,
the way to God.

ISAIAH 8:20
To obtain a revelation and a testimony.

3/2/97

ONE BODY, MY Church. One head, My Pope. One God, My self.

The Church is My body and like all bodies it has only one head and that is My chosen Pope. Chosen to lead My people into the heart of the one true God, the Holy Trinity.

PSALMS 47:4 | *He chose our heritage for us.*

THE PAIN I bore was the pain of love. The pain I bore was the pain of the birth of a new church. The pain I bore was the pain of the reason for My coming.

I came to build a new church. The church that was born in love to live in love. The church that came into being by the sacrifice of My love on the cross. The Church that exists in My love. The Church that should reflect My love. The Church that should offer My love to all. The Church that should share in My sacrificial love every day. The Church that should find its strength in My love. The Church that I founded in My love...The Catholic Church.

IN MY BODY find peace,
   In My body find hope,
   In My body find love,
   My body...the Church.

   ISAIAH 40:1
   Console my people, console them says your Lord.

INTO THE ARMS of the Church you must go
   and you must stay there.

   ISAIAH 24:2 | *Priest and people alike.*

LET THE CHURCH be a sign of truth, stability and love for if it is not then how can it lead people to My love.

   WISDOM 18:19 | *Lest they perish unaware.*

26/7/97

MY FAMILY ON earth,
My body on earth,
My love on earth,

One and the same—My Church.

JOB 16:9 | *The righteous shall hold to his way.*

20/9/97

WITHIN THE CHURCH are people with all the problems that people have. Yet so often it is expected that those in the Church are superhuman with no weaknesses, just perfection itself.

Even the smallest of problems can be made to look so large when it happens within the Church.

The judgement of the world upon the Church is nearly always negative and the world often looks for any mistakes, any weaknesses within the Church so as to destroy it.

If the world would look with love and understanding as it always expects the Church to do, rather than judging and condemning, the world would find a change happening in the hearts of all mankind.

The world should try to remember the Church is filled with goodness, it is just sometimes human weaknesses detract from this.

Without support and help these weaknesses will only grow and the good news of the Church will be hidden beneath these distractions and that will only make the world a worse place not a better one.

ACTS 18:15 | *Do not wish to be a judge on such matters.*

Religious Life

15/5/96

THE CROSS IS carried by many but My priests carry a special burden: This is why it is so important that the lay people help them, support them and love them. Just as I walked Calvary with a heavy burden so do My priests, as Satan attacks them constantly.

Priests, a gift to the world who need to be appreciated for what they are and need to be helped in what they do.

4/8/96

A SHEPHERD, A GUIDE, a bishop...

A shepherd of men who guides home to heaven
My children...this is a bishop.

LUKE 18:28
Then Peter said, 'Lo, we have left all, and followed thee.'

5/8/96

THE BLESSING OF a priest is My blessing, for a priest's hands become Mine when he does My work.

15/9/96

PRIESTS REPRESENT MY love,
Priests represent My mercy,
Priests represent Me...Treasure them.

PSALMS 25:14 | *He affirms his covenant with them.*

27/9/96

IN A PRIEST see My love
    In a priest see My gift to mankind.
    In a priest see a reflection of
    My love which is a gift to mankind.

Priests sometimes falter because like all other humans they have weaknesses but just as priests are expected to forgive and understand others, others should offer the priests the same forgiveness and understanding.

8/10/96

THE JOY IN a priest's heart when he is in love with Me is a joy that can set other hearts alight in My love.

ZECHARIAH 3:1
And the Lord showed me Jesus the high priest.

19/10/96

WOMEN OF GOD have a deep strength within their hearts.
    Women of God have a deep love within their souls.
    Women of God have a deep understanding of life within their spirits.

5/4/97

IN A PRIEST, see love.
    In a priest, see hope.
    In a priest, see Me.

LUKE 10:23
Happy the eyes that see what you see.

13/4/97

IN THE HEART of a priest, I am.
  In the heart of a priest, I love.
  In the heart of a priest, I exist.

5/6/97

PRIESTS—MY BROTHERS, MY servants and My friends.
  Priests—My love, My hope and My light.
  Priests—My image, My reflection and My truth when
  they truly love Me and live for Me.

JOSHUA 17:4 | *To give us a heritage.*

5/8/97

IN A PRIEST see love.
  In a priest see hope.
  In a priest see grace,
  for a priest is a grace of love given in hope.

EZEKIEL 25:1 | *They may know that I am the Lord.*

25/8/97

THE WORDS OF a priest can be words of grace and words of
  true love if the priest believes in Me and what I offer in
  the Sacraments.

DANIEL 12:3
*And those who lead many to justice shall be like the stars
forever.*

WISDOM 19:9 | *Praising you O Lord their deliverer.*

28/8/97

A PRIEST IS A man who first and foremost loves Me. A priest is a man who spends his life in worship of Me. A priest is a man who brings others to love and worship Me.

If a priest is not true to this then he must review his life and change to do as I ask of him otherwise he has no priesthood at all.

JOHN 4:10 | *If you knew the gift of God.*

JEREMIAH 6:15 | *They are.*

LUKE 22:18 | *The blessing.*

EZEKIEL 26:2 | *To the peoples.*

JOHN 12:13
Blessed is he who comes in the name of the Lord.

28/8/97

A RELIGIOUS LIFE IS a life of sacrifice and a life of love, for it is a life that should remind the world of My sacrifice of love. A religious life is a precious gift that many are called to but few truly accept. A religious life is a proclamation of the greatness of God and the importance of God in that person's life.
The religious every day need to ask for the graces and gifts that are needed to keep My love alight in their heart and to keep My love at the centre of their life. The religious every day need to be aware of their weaknesses and how evil attacks these weaknesses in the hope of destroying a vocation. The religious every day need to be immersed in

My body and blood with complete devotion so that they can be strengthened for the times they and others are in need.

SIRACH 15:3
Nourish him with the bread of understanding and give him the water of learning to drink.

....

9/11/97

A man of love who shares his love is what a priest should be. A man of love who lives his love is what a priest should be. A man of love who proclaims his love is what a priest should be...

His love of God.

ESTHER 8:8
So as to render the kingdom undisturbed and peaceful for all men.

15/11/97

BISHOPS ARE SHEPHERDS of the flock, there to lead in faith, in love, in obedience and by example. Bishops have a heavy responsibility to care for the souls of My family. If they rely on themselves they will not succeed but if they rely on Me they will not fail. Bishops sit on a seat that is a gift from heaven and each day they should thank God for that gift.

It is when a bishop remembers that God has given him everything in his life and accepts that by himself he can do nothing, the bishop will find the strength to be an obedient servant of God to shepherd his flock home to heaven.

PSALMS 78:72
He shepherded them with a pure heart with skilled hands he guided them.

Obedience

15/7/97

OBEDIENCE ALWAYS, OBEDIENCE to God and obedience to the Catholic Church.

In this way you will succeed in doing My will.

BARUCH 5:8 | *At God's command.*

15/11/97

OBEDIENCE SHOWS COMPLETE faith.
Obedience shows complete trust.
Obedience shows you are Mine.

When you are obedient to My will, overcoming your own desires and demands, it shows you are completely Mine and that you trust that in Me only what is best will happen.

SIRACH 40:26
Fear of the Lord leaves nothing wanting he who has it need
seek no other support.

Faith

5/1/96

FAITH IS WEAK in times of plenty
and strong in times of need.

5/1/96

A CRIPPLED MAN CAME to Me and his faith was strong.
In his faith he was healed. A healthy man came to
Me and his faith was weak. In his faith he was lost.

The crippled man became whole in God and the healthy
man became lost in the world.

2/2/96

Faith breeds goodness
and goodness leads to heaven.

3/6/96

UNITED IN LOVE with God all is possible.
Believe that and see all happen.

12/6/96

FAITH IS STRONG in times of need.
Faith is weak in times of plenty.
Times of plenty are really times
when there is the most need.

WISDOM 10:8
For, by neglecting the path of wisdom, not only were they
kept from knowledge of the good they actually left the world
a memorial of their folly.

25/8/96

IF YOU TRULY believe in Me all is possible.
If you truly love Me all can happen.
If you truly adore Me all will be.

8/1/97

IN FAITH, IN trust, in hope, know I am there.

16/1/97

IF YOU FEEL lonely I am there.
If you feel lost I am there.
If you feel unloved I am there.

I am always there, just believe.

JEREMIAH 34:3
And thou shalt be delivered into his hand.

10/4/97

THE REMOVAL OF doubt is the beginning of faith.

PSALMS 57:10 | *Your faithfulness.*

4/5/97

TO BE SURE of life turn to Me.
  To be certain of love, come to Me.
  To be firm in faith, reach out to Me.

I am there waiting to help you live your life in faith so that you can come to Me in eternal love.

MATTHEW 12:21 | *In his name the nations will put their hope.*

. . . .

17/6/97

In My arms forever,
  In My heart forever,
  In Me forever...

Those who truly believe.

ISAIAH 45:17
You shall never be put to shame or disgrace.

12/7/97

UNITED IN LOVE,
  United in hope,
  United in truth,

All those who believe in Me.

MARK 11:17
My house shall be called a house of prayer for all people.

24/8/97

ONE FAMILY IN God, those who believe.
One family in God, those who have faith.

One family in God, those who love in God's name and
have the faith to share that love.

ISAIAH 4:2 | *The fruit of the earth.*

Grace

20/2/96

THOSE WHO SHOW thanks to God for His mercy receive the
grace of God's love.
Those who show thanks to God for His love receive the
grace of God's mercy.

2 PETER 3:18
*Go on growing in the grace and in the knowledge of our Lord
and saviour, Jesus Christ.*

16/12/96

TO BECOME FULL of self is a sin, to give selflessly, a grace.

6/2/97

GOD'S GRACES, THERE for all.
God's graces, offered to all.
God's graces, there if you ask.

17/2/97

IN THE GRACE of God all is possible and to be in that grace
you must pray and open your heart to the truth.

13/5/97

GRACE-FILLED DAYS COME with trust in Me.
Grace-filled days come with love of Me.
Grace-filled days come with life for Me.

15/5/97

TO GIVE A friend a gift is expected but
to give a stranger a gift is a grace.

ECCLESIASTICUS 29:12
Deposit generosity in your storerooms.

14/9/97

TO SING THE praises of God is a grace that all can have if they
just open their mouth and try.

When they do, even the hardest voice becomes soft in My
love and becomes a sound of beauty throughout eternity.

MARK 12:11 | *And it is wonderful in our eyes.*

5/10/97

MAKING THE EFFORT to love is what makes you grow in graces. It is when times are difficult, or people are difficult,
and you make an effort only to respond in love, that you
will find many graces granted to you and you will find you
grow in love.

Holiness

15/11/96

HOLINESS, A WAY of life. Forgiveness, a way to holiness.

In a holy life forgiveness becomes part of your life and brings you closer to the truth of life.

22/9/97

DO NOT FEAR your humanity; appreciate it for the gift it is, a gift to help you grow, a gift to help you love, and a gift God gave to you.

PROVERBS 4:22 | *Man's whole being.*

Souls

11/1/97

WHEN YOU LOOK at a flower you appreciate its beauty.
When you smell a flower you appreciate its aroma. When you touch a flower you appreciate its delicate structure.

Souls, like flowers, are beautiful to Me and smell so sweet when they are filled with love. It is My touch that strengthens delicate souls and fills them with My love.

ZEPHANIAH 3:17 | *He will renew you by his love.*

23/1/97

SICKNESS OF BODY is sad indeed,
    Sickness of mind, a tragedy,
    Sickness of soul, an agony.

When the body is sick it is a sadness to the person and his
family. When the mind is sick it can be a tragedy for all
involved. When the soul is sick it is an agony that hurts
the sufferer and those who love him, as they see, unless
he is cured, it will be a never-ending tragedy, and that
truly is sad.

JOB 37:2 | *Listen, oh listen.*

10/12/97

THE FRAGRANCE OF a love that emits from a pure heart is a
delight to Me. The aroma of a spirit submissive to My will
is a joy to Me. The perfume of a soul seeking holiness is a
beautiful gift to Me.

A delightful gift, which I take to the Father, is the soul
seeking holiness and together we reach out in the Holy
Spirit to bring that person to the eternal gift of heaven.

JOEL 1:14 | *Into the house of the Lord.*

Heaven

4/1/96

TO UNDERSTAND A mystery of God is only possible when you reach heaven for then you are pure love. It is your life on earth that helps you reach heaven.

So the earthly life is part of unraveling the mystery, but only a part, not the answer.

22/9/96

THERE ARE MANY paths to God
but I am the only way to heaven.

22/9/96

IN ME ARE the doors to heaven.
In Me is the path to eternal life.

In Me find the path that leads you to the doors of heaven and through Me find them opened.

27/1/97

FOLLOW ME, NO other.
Believe in Me, no other.
Trust Me, no other,
Then come to heaven and no other place.

PSALMS 60:12
With God among us we shall fight like heroes.

14/8/97

IN MY FATHER'S house is love.
　　In My Father's house is peace.
　　In My Father's house is a place for all those who seek it.

MATTHEW 13:43
The righteous will shine like the sun in the kingdom of their father.

....

5/10/97

I give My word to all who pray,
　　　　to all who love Me and to all who
　　　　serve Me that heaven awaits.

HOSEA 6:2 | *To live in his presence.*

10/10/97

WALK WITH ME in love,
　　walk with Me in hope and then
　　walk with Me to heaven.

MALACHI 2:4 | *Because I have a covenant with*

JEREMIAH 6:16 | *your souls.*

Saints

A SAINT IS MADE in heaven but grows on earth.

MATTHEW, A FRIEND of God.
  Matthew, a servant of God.
  Matthew, My friend who served Me well.

  Matthew, a sinner who became a saint, what an example to all! Matthew, a saint who helped sinners, what a gift to all!

  ACTS 13:47
  I have made you a light for the gentiles so that all the world may be saved.

A DAY TO CELEBRATE the love and sacrifices of holy men and women. A day to reflect on the glory they brought to God. A day to start to imitate their lives and by doing so receive the same rewards.

WHEN ST JOSEPH first saw Me his heart was set on fire with love. When St Joseph first held Me his heart exploded in joy. When St Joseph first kissed Me his heart knew the love of God and became one with Mine.

St Joseph, a blessed man who sets an example for all on how to love God and in humility accept God's will into your hearts.

JOB 33:23 | *To remind man where his duty lies.*

....

26/12/96

St Stephen, the first of many.
St Stephen, a friend of God.

St Stephen, the first friend to sacrifice his life for Me and to stand firm until the end in My love.

NEHEMIAH 9:20
You gave them your good spirit to make them wise.

22/10/97

A YOUNG CHILD SHOWED how to love and how to be obedient. A young child showed how to be humble. A young child showed how to be a saint.

A child called Bernadette.

ISAIAH 35:8 | *The holy way.*

1/11/97

The Saints —signs of love.
The Saints—examples of love.
The Saints—enjoy an eternity of love.

LUKE 18:22 | *A treasure in heaven.*

9/11/97

SINNERS ON EARTH can become saints in heaven. Sinners on earth can become guiding lights on the way to heaven. Sinners on earth can become a sign of God's mercy offered to all with heaven as the reward for those who accept it. All mankind are sinners but all mankind can be saints, for there is a grace I offer to all.

A grace that says if you repent, if you change your life to one of loving Me and if you treat your brothers and sisters with love, then the gates of heaven will be opened to you and your sins will be forgiven.

I call all sinners to be saints. They only have to respond to that call.

MATTHEW 7:8
For everyone who asks, receives and the one who seeks finds; and to the one who knocks the door will be opened.

22/11/97

ALL MEN AND women are called to be saints and they can answer this call by making their life an offering of love to Me. For many this is hard to do. That is why so few are proclaimed saints on earth.

For many to love Me as they should seems too hard, a burden to carry but they should look and see without loving Me it is life that becomes the burden and death a sadness.

The call goes out in eternity to all mankind—love Me, live in My love and share My love then you too can be saints who will find life a gift not a burden and death a joy not a sorrow.

EZEKIEL 3:19 | *You shall save your life.*

Angels

22/5/96

An angel is by your side,
To love, to guard and to guide.

An angel watches your life,
To protect and to keep from strife.

An angel sent by Me, to make every moment one of joy and to help your life be happy.

Forgiveness

5/1/96

SCRIBES HAVE WRITTEN of the glory of God.
  Scribes have written of the coming of the Saviour.
  Scribes have written of the defeat of evil.

  Many have read but few believe.
  Many can be saved but few understand.
  Many are the sins but all can be forgiven.

14/3/96

THE SICK NEED healing. The poor need help. The sinners need forgiveness and they can find it all in Me.

15/3/96

FORGIVENESS DOES NOT mean acceptance of wrong. Forgiveness should be given with a true heart that explains what is wrong and what is right. Forgiveness shows your love.

MATTHEW 5:44
Love your enemies and pray for those who persecute you.

1/5/96

FORGIVENESS IS FOUND in My heart, love is found in Me. When you love you forgive and when you love you share in Me.

OBADIAH 15
As you have done to another so to you will it be done.

Forgiveness and love are one,
for when you forgive you love
and when you love you forgive.

I LOVE ALL MANKIND and offer My forgiving love to them. My forgiveness knows no end and so it does not matter what you have done, if you truly repent I will forgive you.
All sins can be forgiven if only forgiveness is truly sought.

LOVE AND FORGIVENESS come hand in hand, for without love it is not true forgiveness and without forgiveness it is not true love.

LOVE THROUGH ADVERSITY.
Forgive through suffering.
Understand through confusion.

In love all adversity can be overcome.
In forgiveness all suffering defeated.
In understanding all confusion cleared.

I am the forgiving love of God that understands all of mankind and offers all to mankind.

PROVERBS 23:26 | *My child give me your heart.*

18/4/97

FORGIVENESS IS PART of loving Me
for when you forgive you reflect My love.

5/8/97

Forgiveness begins and ends with
God, for without God forgiveness is
impossible and without God you cannot be forgiven.

I am the forgiveness of God.
Come to Me and be forgiven,
Come to Me and be loved,
Come to Me and be Mine.

ROMANS 9:15
I will show mercy to whom I will.
I will take pity on whom I will.

28/8/97

IF PEOPLE BEHAVE badly you should not respond in the same
way. Respond with love, understanding and forgiveness
then you respond in Me.

WISDOM 4:10 | *He who pleased God was loved.*

PSALMS 40:12 | *Do not withhold your compassion.*

29/10/97

FORGIVENESS SHOWS STRENGTH of heart
   and love of others.

   2 CORINTHIANS 5:19
   Not counting their trespasses against them.

28/11/97

TO FORGIVE IS important, for if you do not,
   you harden your heart and let love leave you.

   EPHESIANS 4:32
   Forgiving one another as God has forgiven you in Christ.

Mercy

2/6/96

THE DIVINE MERCY, there for all.
   The divine mercy, offered to all.
   The divine mercy, accepted by few.

   PROVERBS 12:15
   In the eyes of a fool the way he goes is right.

8/8/96

GOD'S MERCY, A divine grace.
   God's forgiveness, a divine gift.
   God's love...Divinity.

30/11/96

IN MERCY I forgive,
> In forgiveness I love,
> In love, I am.

Trust

20/11/95

UNDERSTANDING GOD'S WILL is difficult
> so try not to understand try just to follow.

19/12/95

IF YOU PLAN your future with Me as the centre of your life
> then it will be a good plan.

28/12/95

WALKING ACROSS THE mountains one day a follower of Mine
fell and broke his leg. As he cried in pain and anguish I
came to him and comforted him. I saw all of those with
Me waiting expectantly for Me to heal his leg. There was
no doubt, they just believed in Me. I healed his leg and
praised God the Father for His mercy and My followers
did the same.

This is how it should be for all who want My help and love.
They should always be waiting and be expectant of it and
if they just believe then all will be possible.

31/12/95

GIVE ALL OF your worries, all of your cares to Me
> and I will give you all of My love.

17/2/96

THROUGH DIFFICULT TIMES trust.
    Through happy times thank.
    Through eternity be rewarded.

....

15/3/96

Life is a mystery to most, no matter
                    how they try they cannot unravel its
                    secrets. Some however trust in Me
                    and in this trust life becomes obvi-
                    ous.

10/4/96

THE APOSTLES LEARNED to trust in Me but it took the Holy
    Spirit to give them complete trust. My followers, the apos-
    tles of today, are the same; they need to welcome the Holy
    Spirit into their hearts to find that complete trust.

10/5/96

TO TRUST IS not to worry,
    To trust is to give completely,
    To trust is to accept unquestionably,

    Trust...so hard to find but once found such a gift.

    ECCLESIASTICUS 10:5
    A man's success is in the hands of the Lord.

20/5/96

EVEN WHEN IT seems nothing is happening, know it is.
   Often this is when the most happens.

18/6/96

TRUST IN ME,
   Believe in Me,
   Love in Me,
   Then find eternity.

   SONG OF SONGS 8:6
   Set me like a seal on your heart.

4/1/97

TO TRUST ME is all I ask.
   To love Me is all I ask.

   To love Me and trust Me is all that is asked,
   for within that is all.

   JOB 17:5
   Like a man who invites his friends to share his property.

22/1/97

TRUST IS THE key to life. Trust Me and live.

27/1/97

MAKE A CHANGE within, a change that gives your worries to
   Me and that says you trust in Me.

   WISDOM 9:14 | *The reasonings of mortals are unsure.*

23/2/97

A MAN WHO TRUSTS lives in peace.

12/7/97

IN SLEEP FIND peace by praying before you close your eyes. In sleep find peace by asking for My love to surround you and protect you. In sleep find peace by trusting in Me to watch over you.

BARUCH 4:22
I have trusted in the eternal God for your welfare.

15/11/97

WITH TRUST IN Me all is possible.
With trust in Me all can happen.
With trust in Me all can be saved.

ROMANS 10:9 | *Believe in your heart.*

Truth and Honesty

19/12/95

IN FRONT OF all the people who mocked Me, spat on Me and abused Me I never denied the truth. It would have been so easy to lie and to deny the Father and in doing so save My earthly body from its torment.
How could I lie, how could I say that I was not the Son of God, one with the Father, for it is the truth. It is by standing firm in the truth that I defeated evil and it is the same

for everyone. If they keep to the truth they will defeat evil in their lives.

....

5/1/96

In truth all is possible,
in deceit all fails.

7/1/96

KNOWLEDGE COMES WITH truth, the knowledge that God exists. Truth comes with knowledge, the truth that God loves you.

To know that God loves you and because of His love you exist, brings truth into your life.

29/1/96

IT IS TRUE I love all mankind. It is true I love to forgive. It is true I love to save. It is true I love to share. It is true I love to take care. It is true I am God who loves all mankind and I offer My forgiveness to all in love.

I gave My life to save all of My children and I long to share My love in eternity with them where I will care for their souls forever.

4/2/96

SPEAK WITH LOVE but speak the truth.

26/2/96

SIN WILL BE defeated when the truth is accepted. To accept the truth means to deny evil and to deny evil is to defeat sin.

8/4/96

THE LOVE OF God is everything and in the love of God everything is found. The love of God is truth and in the love of God truth is found. The love of God is hope and in the love of God hope is found.

I am the love of God.
In Me find everything,
in Me find hope and
in Me find the truth.

JEREMIAH INTRODUCTION IN JERUSALEM BIBLE.
Line 10: The truth of his message was eventually proved by history.

16/4/96

THE TRUTH, ALWAYS the truth.
Truth defeats evil.

Truth overcomes sins.
Truth, the strength of God.

Truth, inside all but denied by many.
Truth, the way to live.

Truth, eternal...
The truth of God.

2/6/96

In truth you grow.
In truth you develop.
In truth you become your true self.

I am the truth, find yourself in Me.

28/6/96

A FISH IN A pond only knows the world around it; there is no understanding of existence other than this. Many in the world are the same. They only understand what they see around them, what they can touch; anything else is often not even considered.

Like the fish, ignorant of all else, many do not search beyond their immediate environment and because of this they deny so much. This denial does not stop all else being true, it just stops many accepting the truth.

1/7/96

AFRAID OF BEING loved,
Afraid of being wanted,
Afraid of being true.

Most of mankind are afraid of being loved by God, for they know what is wanted of them in God's love and the truth hurts when you have been away from it for so long.

ISAIAH 57:18
But I will heal him and console him.
I will comfort him to the full.

24/7/96

BE TRUTHFUL, BE honest, and be sincere in all you do.

20/8/96

THE JOY OF love,
    The love of God.

    The truth of love,
    The truth of God.

    The hope of love,
    The hope of God.

    I am, I was and I always will be the love that brings hope
    to those who seek the truth.

14/11/96

THE TRUTH ALWAYS wins,
    the truth never changes,
    the truth is eternal.

    I am the truth.

23/12/96

THE TRUTH, ALWAYS the truth.
    Honesty, always honesty.
    Justice, always justice.

    If these are not upheld what an example for the young, an
    example that condones sin.

ECCLESIASTICUS 5:10 |*Be steady in your convictions.*

13/1/97

IN TRUTH YOU stand, in deceit you fall.

ISAIAH 66:16 | *The victims of Yahweh will be many.*

13/2/97

Truth always ... sin never.

9/5/97

DO NOT DENY the truth even a little
for then it is not the truth.

1 CORINTHIANS 2:10
The very things God has revealed.

16/5/97

The truth is nothing to fear,
it should be embraced;
for in the truth I am.

EZRA 1:5
*In fact all whose spirit had
been roused by God.*

21/6/97

SPEAK THE TRUTH always and always in kindness.

27/10/97

IN THE WORLD today there are many different interpretations of the truth. Many of these are interpretations designed to change the truth and then it is the truth no more.
I am the truth Who, with the Father and the Holy Spirit, never changes. My truth is clear, My truth is obvious but so often My truth is denied.

JONAH 2:9
Those who worship vain idols forsake their source of mercy.

25/11/97

BEING HONEST IS a requisite if you profess to love Me and claim to do My will, for without honesty you only do the will of evil and show you love yourself more than Me.

The Life of Jesus

12/12/95

AS I WALKED through the desert and then climbed the mountain I thought of the love that was wasted throughout the world. The love that could bring peace and joy to all, the love that was the answer to all of mankind's needs, the love that is God.
I saw so many who did not even consider for a moment what was there for them in the love they denied. I felt sad

that so many did not understand what God offered them in His love.

The Father sent Me to show mankind that God's love is real and it is there for all.

As I walked I opened My heart to the world and let My mercy fill the air and I continued to do so throughout My life on earth and I continue to do so throughout eternity.

The mercy of God is here for all, I offer it to all and all I ask in return is love.

8/2/96

THE WORDS, THE truth, the love.
The actions, the gifts, the love.
The sacrifice, the redemption, the love.

My life!

JOHN 11:25
I am the resurrection, if anyone believes in me, even though he dies he will live, and whoever lives and believes in me will never die.

5/8/96

AT THE JUNCTION of the roads there are many ways to walk. Some lead you away from your destination. Some are long and difficult roads which often many give up on and fall by the wayside.

There is one path however that never leads you away. A path that at the beginning may seem long but once you have walked it you realize it was the shortest and quickest way home. A path which has a map to guide you along it. A path that is the path of life.

I am that path and in My life I laid out before mankind the way to walk, the way home to heaven, the way of God.

PSALMS 119
Blessed are the undefiled in the way, who walk in the law of the Lord.

4/1/97

MY LIFE, AN example for all on how to live, how to love and how to give. My life, the answer to all things... My life.

3/9/97

IN MY LIFE you see how all mankind should try to be.
In My life you see how all mankind should live
if they want to be free.
In My life you see how all mankind should love
if they want to be loved eternally.

A sign for all, a guidance for all,
and a way to heaven for all; My life.

1 SAMUEL 12:24
Keep in mind all the great things he has done among you.

16/11/97

MY LIFE SHOWS all how to live.
My life shows all how to overcome sin.
My life shows all how to be assured a place in heaven.

ISAIAH 45:22 | *For I am God.*

BARUCH 4:22 | *Your eternal saviour.*

17/11/97

IN MY LIFE you will see love.
　　In My life you will see forgiveness.
　　In My life you will see how your life must be.

ISAIAH 30:26 | *Like the light.*

Living in God

6/4/96

JOYFUL LOVE, GLORIOUS love, The love of God.
　　True life, Fruitful life, The life of God.
　　Happy times, Wonderful times, The times of God.

The love of God brings you to life in God. Life in God makes you want to spend time with God to deepen your love of God.

26/6/96

Love, hope, charity,
　　peace, joy...all found in Me
　　if only they are sought.

30/7/96

LOVE, PEACE AND tranquility, all gifts of God, all there for those who seek them.

4/8/96

IN GOD...TRUST,
    In God...love,
    In God...give.

26/8/96

IN ME FIND life,
    In Me find love,
    In Me find God.

    MARK 13:21 | *Look here he is the Messiah.*

18/1/97

TO THINK OF Me is to be with Me.

    ECCLESIASTICUS 34:17
    He revives the spirit and brightens the eyes.

26/1/97

PRESENCE OF MIND,
    Presence of heart,
    Presence of soul.

    I am that presence, the presence of love.

    ESTHER 1:16 | *In the presence of the king.*

14/2/97

DO NOT CRITICIZE others; understand them.
    Do not condemn others; help them.
    Do not judge others; pray for them.

    There is no other way if you love Me.

17/2/97

LET YOUR MIND wander in My love.
    Let your soul join with Me.
    Let your heart be united in Mine.

Then together we can love, love, love.

7/3/97

IN YOUR WORDS, love.
    In your in actions, love.
    In your thoughts, love.

Then you live in Me.

11/3/97

THINK IN LOVE, act in love, then be in love...My love.

JOHN 1:4 | *All that came to be had life in him.*

14/3/97

LOVE IS THE greatest gift you can have, for
    I am love and in Me your life becomes complete.

JEREMIAH 4:5 | *Shout the message aloud.*

20/4/97

JUST THINK OF Me and I am there.
    Just be aware of Me and I am there.
    Just come to Me and I am there.

There for all in love and in hope.

18/5/97

IN MY LOVE all should live
 then they would find true life.

. . . .

25/6/97

In Me you live,
  without Me, you die.

28/6/97

EACH BREATH,
 Each thought,
 Each word,
 For Me.

 Each moment,
 Each heartbeat,
 Each action,
 For Me.

 Each person,
 Each church,
 Each country,
 For Me.

Then each day will be a day in paradise.

PROVERBS 8:21 | *Enriching those who love me.*

12/7/97

A RIVER FLOWS DOWN from the mountains to the sea. Along the way it brings life wherever it goes.

So it is from heaven that a river flows down to earth bringing with it; life for all souls it touches. I am that river, reach out and touch Me and find eternal life.

WISDOM 3:1 | *The souls of the just are in the hand of God.*

12/7/97

VISIONS OF LOVE, those who love God.

Visions of joy, those who share this love.

Visions of hope, those who live this love.

MALACHI 1:11 | *A pure offering.*

27/8/97

IF YOU ARE to live in My love then you must not hold anger or resentment on your heart. You must not hold onto the hurt you feel when others are insensitive to your needs. You must not be upset by the way others react to your offer of love.

You must only love and you must always forgive.

26/8/97

BROTHERS IN ME is how all men should be. Brothers in My arms is how all men can be. Brothers in eternal love is how all men were created to be. All men should seek to be brothers in Me and then they will find eternal life in My love can be theirs.

JEREMIAH 6:11 | *Yes all will be taken.*

27/8/97

LOVE IS THE only way to live.
Love is the only way to give.

Love is the only way to live your life and in love you will find that you want to give yourself completely to Me for I am love.

30/8/97

MAKE EACH MOMENT a moment of love by thinking of Me.

ACTS 2:25 | *I saw the Lord ever before me.*

2/11/97

IN YOUR WORDS be kind.
In your words be forgiving.
In your words be loving.

Then I am in your words.

ZECHERIAH 13:9 | *And I will refine them.*

11/12/97

TO SHARE EVERY moment with Me is to truly love Me. To live every moment with Me is to truly love Me. To see every moment as being a moment with Me is to truly love Me.

Every moment can be a moment of love when you live with Me and share your life with Me. It is then you will see the joy of truly loving Me.

MICAH 4:5 | *Walk in the name of the Lord.*

Imitating the Lord

5/12/95

To shine in the dark often means to suffer.
To love where there is hate often means pain.
To give where there is selfishness often means to hurt.

The way of love is a painful way but it is through this that your spirit can shine as it glorifies God.

17/12/95

When your family takes all
you have to give and expects
to give nothing in return
and when they abuse you when
you ask for what is due then
you know some of the pain
I feel each time a child of God
treats Me so.

22/12/95

One day a man came to Me and asked, 'How can You claim to be the Son of God, for Your father was a carpenter?' Even though he had seen many miracles, heard only words of God's love, he could not believe, for his mind could not accept what it could not understand.

It hurt Me when people closed their eyes and their hearts to the truth and only believed in what they thought was true. Today it is the same no matter how much I show My love still many will not accept it.

Today when I shower the world with My gifts and give My graces to many, those who do not understand deny them. Even those who profess their love for Me often refuse to accept My will for it does not fit into their expectations.

Remember that I faced this in My life on earth and that you will face it in your life for Me on earth. See it as sharing in My suffering and offer it to Me as a gift of love.

9/2/96

MY FRIENDSHIP EXTENDS to all and so must yours.
My help is for all and so must yours be.
My love is for all and so must yours be.

When you do this you follow Me and do My will.

21/3/96

A FOLLOWER OF MINE loves, understands and tries to help.
A follower of Mine never condemns, judges or rejects his fellow man.

A follower of Mine shows the truth to those who do not understand it, brings love to those who need it, and helps those who are lost find the way.

30/3/96

SHOW THANKS,
Show love,
Show forgiveness...always.

17/5/96

SEE WITH EYES of love.
> Feel with a heart of love.
> Give with a spirit of love.

Do this and become a reflection of My love.

DEUTERONOMY 10:12
To follow all his ways, to love him, to serve Yahweh your God with all your heart and soul.

20/6/96

SHOW LOVE IN your words,
> Show love in your actions,
> Show love in your heart.

....

5/10/96

Being honest, being kind,
being loving
is being a follower of Mine.

12/12/96

PATIENCE, KINDNESS, UNDERSTANDING,
> forgiveness and love...
> This is My way; make it yours.

ROMANS 7:7 | *You shall not covet.*

10/3/97

REMEMBER HOW I loved when I was on earth
and try to do the same.

....

13/3/97

Remember, act wisely,
act in love and
act with no malice.

JEREMIAH 50:21 | *Do everything I have.*

20/3/97

BE FRIENDLY,
Be loving,
Be truthful,
Be honest,
Be open,
Be joy-filled,
Be hope-filled,

Then be a reflection of Me.

25/3/97

DO NOT BE selfish. Do not be only concerned for yourself. Do
not be filled with your own importance.

Consider others as I did. Love others as I did. Be kind to
others as I was when I lived on earth, then you live as I
ask you to.

28/4/97

GENTLENESS IS MY way, caring is My way,
  loving is My way, truth is My way,
  understanding is My way, forgiving is My way,
  mercy is My way,

These are My ways, make them yours.

ISAIAH 48:17
I, Yahweh, your God, teach you what is good for you.

9/5/97

WHEN YOU SEE wrong stand against it,
  When you see right praise it.

ECCLESIASTICUS 15:9
Praise is unseemly in a sinner's mouth.

9/7/97

RESPOND TO THE plight of others in prayer, in kindness and
in love. Then you respond how I want you to.

WISDOM 19:22
*Unfailing you stood by them in every time and
circumstance.*

13/10/97

LOVE SHOULD BE in every breath, every heartbeat
  and every thought if you want to imitate Me.

ECCLESIASTICUS 3:8 | *A time to love.*

EPHESIANS 5:2 | *And live in love.*

Working for God

23/12/95

AN ELDER IN the temple one day said to Me, 'You blas-
pheme, You call Yourself the Son of God, You come from
the devil.'

How could it be possible that a man who had work long
and hard for God did not know God?

It is because often in the work the reason for it is forgotten, often in the work hearts become closed to all except
what they see as the work. All those who work for God
must remember why they work. It should be to spread
God's love and to magnify God's glory.

In the work they do these people should remember that
they are humble servants of God and that God's will is
the work they do. When this is forgotten pride takes its
place and it is in pride that even those who want to do
God's will deny God.

Remember always the work is important but it is the reason for it that is the true goal and that reason is loving
God, obeying God and trusting completely in God.

3/1/96

AS THORNS TEAR the skin so does rejection tear the heart. As
nails pierce the body so does unjust criticism pierce the
heart. As a spear pierced My heart so does the rejection
of My love and the unjust criticism of those whose only
wish is to do My work.

2/3/96

TO DO MY work takes courage, the courage of love.
To do My work takes strength, the strength of faith.
To do My work takes perseverance, the perseverance
of hope.

Faith, hope and love, all found in Me, all found in the Sacraments and all found in God's mercy.

2/8/96

MY WORK DEMANDS only love, trust and obedience; in these
all is possible.

MICAH 5:4 | *With the power of Yahweh.*

27/9/96

SERVANTS OF GOD become targets of Satan.
Servants of God can succumb to evil just as others can.

Servants of God need help and forgiveness from those
they serve in the name of God.

4/11/96

To help others come to Me,
be loving and always try to
understand how others have
weaknesses just as you do.

29/6/97

SERVANTS OF GOD become saints in heaven.

DANIEL 9:27 | *He will make a firm covenant with many.*

4/9/97

TO WORK IN love makes work a joy.
   To work in hope makes work a challenge.
   To work in faith makes work worthwhile.

Doing work for Me means loving, and in faith, hoping My
will be done.

JEREMIAH 22:16
Is this not true knowledge of me says the Lord.

7/10/97

WHEN KINDNESS AND caring shine, then hearts melt
   and souls are touched to become Mine.
   When gentleness and love abound, then this is
   when the lost are found.
   When forgiveness and mercy are spoken, this is
   when those asleep are woken.

15/10/97

IN THE SERVICE of God you must be prepared at all times to
   be called upon and to answer, for in My service you are
   always needed.

MALACHI 1:11 | *Sacrifice to my name.*

Commitment

4/12/95

TAKE YOUR HEART and place it in Mine, then we are one.
Take your spirit and fill it with Mine, then we are one.
Take your life and give it to Me, then we are one.

26/12/95

WHEN A MAN commits his life to Me he gives Me the greatest gift he has. His life is held deep in My heart and every moment his heart beats it is in union with Mine.

27/12/95

WHEN YOU OFFER Me your love you give Me the greatest gift you can, yourself. When you offer Me your soul, you give Me the greatest treasure you have, yourself. When you offer Me yourself I offer you Myself and together we unite in love.

12/4/96

Be loving, be kind, be at peace, be Mine.

8/6/96

PUT YOUR HAND in Mine and let Me lead you.
Put your heart in Mine and let Me love you.
Put yourself in Me and let Me lead you to My love.

22//7/96

TO LOVE ME with your whole heart,
    To love Me with your complete self,
    To love Me with your entire life.

This is how to love Me.

30/7/96

PLACE ALL YOUR cares in My hands.
    Place all your concerns in My hands.
    Place all your life in My hands.

Then see how I care for you, how I am concerned for you
and how I will bring you to eternal life.

PSALMS 78:35
*Remembering that God was their rock, God the Most High,
their redeemer.*

....

3/12/96

A man who commits himself to My work
    is a man who commits himself to
    love.

    ECCLESIASTICUS 9:9
    It kindles desire like a flame.

MAKE EACH MOMENT Mine then
each moment will shine with love.

PROVERBS 4:12
When you walk your step will not be impeded.

LOVE ME WITH a passion.
Share Me with a passion.
And find Me in My passion.

JOHN 2:11 | *And so revealed his glory.*

MAKE YOUR TIME My time.
Make your heart My heart.
Make your life My life.

Then I will make you Mine.

WHEN YOU MAKE your heart Mine
I make My heart yours.
When you make your life Mine
I make My life shine in yours.
When you make your spirit Mine
I make My spirit fill yours.

When you give to Me I return to you more than you could
ever know and more than you could ever need so that you
can share with others.

Perseverance

14/11/96

PERSEVERANCE IS A sign of love.
Perseverance is a sign of faith.

Perseverance is a sign of your love for Me
and it shows how deep is your faith.

DANIEL 4:3 | *How great are his signs.*

True Love

25/11/95

LOVE MAKES ALL problems
seem insignificant,
for love overcomes all.

30/11/95

WHEN YOU SHARE your love it grows.

8/12/95

DO NOT FORCE yourself upon others; only gently embrace
them with your love. Love is to be gentle, to understand
others and to respect others.

27/12/95

SPEAK IN LOVE,
Act in love,
Give in love.

Then you speak, act and give in Me.

30/12/95

WHEN YOU ARE in love every moment is a joy.
When you are in love every moment is a gift.
When you are in love everything is wonderful.

I am love and when you are in Me every moment is a joyful gift of love that makes life wonderful.

30/12/95

CRITICISM SHOULD ONLY be given with love
or it is not true criticism.

30/12/95

TO REJOICE IN My love means to rejoice
when others are filled with My love.
To rejoice in My love means to rejoice
when others accept My love.
To rejoice in My love is to rejoice
when others give their love to Me.

1/1/96

ISN'T LOVE WONDERFUL?
A gift to treasure, a gift to look upon and enjoy...

My gift to you.

5/1/96

IN YOUR EYES have love.
  In your heart be love.
  In your life show love.

23/1/96

LOVE IS THE power that drives your soul and
  your soul is the power that guides you heart.

27/1/96

LOVE OVERCOMES ALL.
  Love unites all.
  Love strengthens all.

I am love and in Me find the strength to overcome evil to be united with Me in eternity.

4/2/96

WITH LOVE, ALL differences become as nothing, for love accepts differences. With love, all people become brothers and sisters, for love makes all one family. With love, all hardships can become joys, for love makes them insignificant.

....

9/2/96

In love find joy, in love find peace,
  in love find hope.
  I am love so find them in Me.

13/2/96

CERTAINTY IN LOVE is the strength you need. When you are certain you love Me and I love you, you cannot be defeated. Find that certainty for it is true.

EZEKIEL 37:14
And I shall put my spirit in you, and you will live.

29/2/96

There is a river, a river of love.
There is a river, a river of forgiveness.
There is a river, a river of mercy.

The river that flows from My side offers My love and forgiveness to all in need of God's mercy.

2/3/96

MY LOVE IS there for all.
My heart is open to all.
My forgiveness is offered to all.

Accept My love from My open heart and receive My forgiveness.

9/3/96

LOVE IS GIVEN freely without expectations of rewards.
Love is offered to all with no exceptions.
Love is there, it only has to be accepted.

10/3/96

LOVE—A SMALL WORD that means so much.
Love—a wonderful gift that is offered to all.
Love—a rose from My heart placed into yours.

PROVERBS 10:2
The blessing of Yahweh is what brings riches.

. . . .

18/3/96

It is in each person... My love.
It is for each person... My love.
It is offered to each person...My love.

If they only knew what was truly offered then each
person would reach out and accept
My love.

30/3/96

LOVE IS A sharing of hearts.
Love is a giving of self.
Love is a longing to help.

Love is Me.

31/3/96

SEE IN EACH person My love and
then give them your love.

4/4/96

WITHIN THE TABERNACLE find life.
On the cross find salvation.

In Me find love.

8/4/96

TO LOVE MEANS to give completely.
To love means to accept completely.
To love means to want completely.

To give yourself completely to God, to accept God's wishes for you, and to want to please God, always show true love, the love of God.

PSALMS 107:1 | *His love is everlasting.*

29/4/96

TO WALK MY path, love.
To come to heaven, love.
To do My will, love.
Love is the answer to all...

I am love.

PSALM 21:8 | *Through the love of the Lord.*

30/4/96

MY WORK, MY love,
My people, My love,
My Church, My love,
My love, the future.

29/5/96

LOVE IS A gift, which, when it is nurtured,
grows to become a treasure.

....

6/8/96

To be true to Me, love.
Love all with a deep love
that denies none and helps all.

29/9/96

LOVE MAKES ALLOWANCES for the weaknesses of others. Love means to help others overcome their weaknesses. Love means to see the good in others and to help them grow in goodness. Love means forgiving others. Love means offering others your helping hand in difficult moments. Love means showing others how to live the life they were created for. Love means sharing your life with others. Love means giving freely, expecting no reward except that which helps your love to grow. Love means accepting that others make mistakes as you do but helping them to see their mistakes and overcoming them. Love means accepting the help that you need in overcoming your mistakes and weaknesses.

Love means living, for love created life.

EZEKIEL 37:25 | *They will live in it.*

15/11/96

TREAT ALL WITH love then be a treat to all.

13/12/96

IN LOVE ALL is possible.
  In love all can be.
  In love all should be.

4/1/97

JOYFUL LOVE,
  Glorious love,
  God's love.

4/1/97

I AM, I WAS and I will be love forever.

8/1/97

MY LOVE FOR you is eternal.
  My love for you is peaceful.
  My love for you is strengthening.

  In My love find peace of mind, strength of heart and eternal rest for your soul.

  ECCLESIASTICUS 39:19
  Blessing the Lord for all his works.

18/1/97

IN COMPLETE LOVE of God you love everyone.
  In complete love of God you become complete.
  In complete love of God you find Me.

26/1/97

TO SHOW CONCERN for others is to show love.

WISDOM 18:9
The saints would share the same blessings and dangers alike.

12/2/97

LOVE IS MISUNDERSTOOD by many, for they believe love is only for their family and friends. Many believe love is just a feeling between a man and a woman, a feeling that only they can share. Many believe love is a personal emotion that has little to do with facts and reality. Many believe that love is another way of saying desire. Many even believe love does not exist.

The reality is that love does exist, that is a fact. Love is a grace given to mankind to share with each other. Love is the gift of God by which all things were created. Love is the way that all should express their lives through their actions. Love is the only way to heaven. Love is the life that seems elusive to so many. Love is the answer to mankind's problems. Love is everywhere if only people would look with eyes opened in truth.

I am love and that is the truth. I am the only way to heaven there is no other. I am the love of God through which all was created and through which all must return if they truly seek eternal happiness. I am the truth of love that mankind needs to understand if it is to exist with God in eternity. I am the love that all hearts need to be filled with if they seek the truth.

JEREMIAH 9:12 | *Who is wise enough to understand this?*

29/4/97

REMEMBER, LOVE ALWAYS, condemn never.

6/5/97

COME TO ME in love and receive My love in return.

....

21/6/97

Love is a small word but a word that
contains everything you need in it,
for I am love and in Me is everything.

1 THESSALONIANS 3:9
*God himself has taught you to love one
another.*

16/7/97

WHEN YOU TALK to others
always speak with words of love,
there is never a reason not to.

PSALMS 61:4
A tower of strength against the foe.

7/8/97

THE LOVE OF others comes from the love of God.

JONAH 2:7 | *O Lord my God.*

9/8/97

LOVE MEANS UNDERSTANDING, caring and forgiving.
Love means sharing, hoping and trusting.
Love means giving, helping and being kind.

How can you love if you do not do these.

MATTHEW 7:20 | *So by their fruits you will know them.*

. . . .

23/9/97

Show love, offer love
and be love to all.

PSALMS 142:4 | *You know my path.*

8/10/97

MANY CLAIM MY love,
many seek My love,
many want My love...

And there is enough for all.

ISAIAH 9:19 | *They are hungry.*

8/11/97

REMEMBER TRUE LOVE denies no one, true love is offered to
all and true love is only possible in Me.

ISAIAH 14:2 | *The Lord's soil.*

7/12/97

MANY SEARCH FOR love in their lives but unless
they find Me they will never find true love.

TITUS 3:4 | *Love of God our Saviour.*

The Heart

25/11/95

LET IT SHINE from your heart, true love of God.
Let it shine from your soul, true faith in God.
Let it shine from within your heart to fill the
hearts and souls of your brothers and sisters.

6/12/95

HEART OF GOD, love of God.
Grace of God, love of God.
Gift of God, love of God.

There for all who ask.

8/1/96

AMAZING IS THE love of God when it is accepted into a heart.
Wondrous is the love of God when it is embraced by a
humble person. Incredible are the results when God's love
is welcomed into a heart with humble acceptance.

ACTS 8:13
*Astonished when he saw the wonders and great miracles that
took place.*

8/1/96

SEE FROM THE heart,
> Feel from the soul,
> Love from the grace of God.

24/1/96

IN YOUR HEART feel Me,
> In your mind accept Me,
> In your soul love Me.

ZECHARIAH 10:7 | *Their heart shall rejoice in the Lord.*

29/1/96

HEARTS FULL OF love unite to become joyful.
> Hearts full of peace unite to become blissful.
> Hearts full of love unite in peaceful joy to become bliss-
> fully part of Me.

....

22/2/96

A heart opened to My love
> is a heart open to all for I love all.
> A heart open to Me
> is open to all as I am open to all.
> A heart given to Me
> is given to all for I give to all.

28/2/96

TEARS FROM THE heart are tears of love.

5/3/96

THE HEART OF God is a heart of giving.
The heart of God is a heart of loving.
The heart of God is a heart of friendship.

All hearts filled with My love become as this.

1 JOHN 4:21
Anyone who loves God must also love his brothers.

....

26/3/96

Peoples' hearts are foolish at times,
foolish when they are closed to Me.

29/3/96

MY HEART IS full of joy,
My heart is full of love,
My heart is full of hope.

My heart waits to fill My children with joy that brings
hope for a future of love.

16/4/96

IN MY HEART find yourself,
In My heart find peace,
In My heart find love.

When you place your heart in Mine you find peaceful love
that helps you to understand who you truly are.

26/6/96

IN THE HEART of God is all you desire.
In the heart of God is all you need.

In the heart of God find all you need and could ever desire, find it in Me for I am the sacred heart of God.

26/6/96

AN OPEN BOOK can easily be read if you know how to read.
An open heart can easily be loved if you know how to love.

An open heart is like an open book, the love within it can be easily seen and read if you know how to. How? In love and in Me.

1/7/96

HEARTS ARE MADE of love to be love.
Hearts are made of joy to be joy.
Hearts are made of kindness to be kind.

In a kind heart love grows and brings joy to others.
Become a kind heart and love joyfully for Me.

10/7/96

A KIND HEART SHINES through,
A kind heart overcomes,
A kind heart warms others.

Always be kind and always from your heart.

12/7/96

LOVE IS THE strength of your heart.

14/7/96

PEACE AND LOVE,
Grace and gifts,
Life and eternity.

All found in My heart where there is room for all.

16//7/96

WHEN YOU LOOK into the eyes of another look with your heart and you will see theirs.

ECCLESIASTICUS 11:4 | *Though hidden from mankind.*

28/7/96

IN EACH PERSON'S heart is a longing to be loved.
In each person's heart is a need to be wanted.
In each person's heart is a searching for love, a love
that fills their needs and shows they are wanted.

The love they seek is My love if only they would accept it.

MATTHEW 5:4 | *They shall have the earth for their heritage.*

18/10/96

KINDNESS IN YOUR heart, forgiveness in your soul, understanding in your mind.

Have these and have peace of mind that opens your heart to understand the needs of others and the reason for living.

13/11/96

THE QUIET OF heart is found in Me.

18/11/96

IT BRINGS JOY to My heart to see those who love Me.
It brings joy to My heart to see those who care for Me.

It brings joy to My heart to see those, who in humble love
care about the way I am ignored.

4/1/97

A HEART OF LOVE,
A heart of joy,
A heart of hope,

Brings gladness to all.

PSALMS 119: 76 | *Let your love comfort me.*

....

20/1/97

A heart of love, a heart of peace,
a heart of trust,
this is a heart that follows Me.

PSALMS 59:17 | *The God who loves me.*

21/1/97

AN OPEN HEART, an honest heart, a loving heart...
This is the heart of a true follower of Mine.

2 CHRONICLES 20:12 | *Given us as our inheritance.*

8/3/97

Let your heart be free in My love.
Let your soul be free in My spirit.
Let your self be free in eternity.

Open your heart and fill your soul
with Me then find your spirit in
eternal bliss with Me.

ECCLESIASTICUS 15:6
He will find happiness and a crown of joy.

12/3/97

MAKE A WELCOME in your heart for everyone you meet
then you make a welcome for Me.

9/4/97

LET LOVE REIGN in your heart.
Let love live in your heart.
Let love be in your heart.

Then be in Me and live in My reign of love.

ECCLESIASTICUS 11:17
The Lord's gift remains constant to the devout.

22/5/97

A HEART OF LOVE forgives,
A heart of love cares,
A heart of love understands.

I am the heart of love and I forgive all who ask, for I understand their weaknesses and I care for their souls.

JEREMIAH 22:3
Deliver him that is oppressed out of the hand of the oppressor.

25/6/97

IMPRESS UPON YOUR heart to love others and in that love to feel no jealousy or resentment. Love means to encourage, to feel joy at the success of others, and to be happy when you see good done.

1 CORINTHIANS 1:10
I urge you brothers in the name of the Lord Jesus Christ, that all of you agree in what you say, and that there be no divisions among you, but that you be united in the same mind and the same purpose.

26/7/97

THERE IS PEACE in My heart for those who want it and there is hope in the hearts of those who seek it.

LUKE 18:42 | *Your faith has saved you.*

9/8/97

THOSE WHOSE HEARTS are pure are so because of My love. Those whose hearts are full of love are so because of My love. Those whose hearts are full of peace are so because of My love.

My love only brings a peaceful heart filled with My pure love.

11/8/97

IN FERTILE SOIL love grows. In fertile soil love produces fruit. In fertile soil love becomes strong.

A heart can be fertile by being true to its creator and by living the commandments its creator gave.

JEREMIAH 24:7 | *With their whole heart.*

30/8/97

WHEN A FRIEND turns from Me it hurts but know that many who turn away return because My love remains in their heart.

PSALMS 91:16
With length of days I will satisfy them and show them My saving power.

7/9/97

IN MOST HEARTS love resides; it is only that sometimes behind fear and pride it hides. In most hearts is the desire for love; it is only that sometimes it is hidden behind the fear of being rejected and the fear of being hurt. In most hearts is the wish to love; it is only that sometimes the thoughts of self prevent the reaching out to others and the helping of those in need.

To set the love free you just need to make the effort and you only need to ask for My help and it is there for you.

2 SAMUEL 22:17
He reached out from on high and grasped me.

7/9/97

IF YOU CANNOT speak in love then try not to speak, for one
wrong word can break a heart.

SIRACH 46:15 | *His words proved him true.*

13/9/97

IN THE HEART of all mankind is the desire for love.
In the heart of all mankind is the desire for peace.
In the heart of all mankind is the desire for
contentment.

So why does mankind keep turning away from Me, for I
am love and all I bring is peace and contentment in life.

SONG OF SONGS 1:12 | *The King's banquet.*

27/9/97

BE KIND IN your words and thoughtful in your heart.

27/9/97

TAKING THE OPPORTUNITY to apologize when you make a
mistake is an opportunity many ignore. It is by taking it
you show the strength of your heart.

19/10/97

A LONELY HEART NEEDS love. A lonely heart needs caring.
A lonely heart needs healing.
Find it all in Me.

ISAIAH 17:10 | *Your saviour*

JEREMIAH 39:22 | *Your good friend.*

22/10/97

TO PLACE YOUR heart in Mine means to love, regardless of circumstance, regardless of position and regardless of opposition.

In My heart there is only love and if you are truly one with Me you must be the same.

TOBIT 13:14 | *Happy are those who love.*

28/10/97

TO SEARCH FOR love is a desire in all hearts, it is just that sometimes the mind clouds this desire.
To search for love is a longing that is in all hearts, but sometimes this longing is buried under hurt, under pain. To search for love is a desire that is given when each person is created, a desire that leads to Me when the mind is not allowed to confuse the longing inside to come to God.

PSALMS 7:10 | *Who tries hearts and minds.*

28/11/97

IN MY HEART are many chambers each one full of My love and each one full of My joy. When you enter into My heart you will find these awaiting and in each you will find what you could have never imagined. You will find divinity embracing and loving you and you will find eternal peace.

My heart is open to all just look in love and you will find it.

SIRACH 51:23 | *Take up lodging.*

29/11/97

IN YOUR HEART find peace by placing My heart there.

JEREMIAH 51:62 | *Dwell in it.*

1/12/97

WITH LOVE IN your heart you cannot be defeated.
With love in your heart you cannot be the loser.

With love in your heart you have the victory, for I am love
and I have already won.

1 JOHN 3:11
This is the message you have heard from the beginning.

7/12/97

In My heart I have a place for all people
regardless of who they are or what
they have done.
All they need to do is truly seek My
love in repentance and My heart
awaits to fill them with My love.

PSALMS 62:11 *Set your heart upon it.*

Sharing

I **LOOK UPON THOSE** who love Me as My true disciples. Even
if they keep this love privately between Myself and them
I treasure this love. I ask all of these though to look within and see it is a love to be shared, a love that is for all.

If they look upon their love for Me and Mine for them as
only ours and no one else should share it, or have a simi-
lar love, then it is not true love.

If however they feel embarrassed, frightened or even un-
worthy to show this love then they should see that the
love we have will be strengthened not destroyed if they
overcome these barriers and express their love freely. It
is by sharing and showing their love for Me that others
can come to know Me and be saved. This is the true love
I long all to have.

TO **SHARE IN** My love means to share in My suffering.
To share in My suffering means to share in saving souls.

To share in saving souls means to share in My eternal
glory.

TO **SHARE WITH** Me is to share with others.
When you share with others you share with Me.

9/3/96

GIFTS SHARED BRING wonderful results.
    Gifts kept for yourself bring only pride.

10/5/96

A JOY TO BEHOLD, the love of God in action.
    A grace to strengthen, the love of God proclaimed.
    A gift to help, the love of God shared.

    ZACHARIAH 9:17
    What joy and what beauty shall be theirs.

....

13/6/96

To share My love
    is to grow in My love.

2/7/96

I HAVE SO MUCH to give,
    I have so much to offer,
    I have so much to share.

    I offer My love in a giving that asks for you to share what
    you receive.

31/8/96

IN LOVE I give, In love I offer,
    In love receive and in love, share.

8/12/96

THE SHARING OF graces,
    The sharing of gifts,
    The sharing of love....

The way of God.

ZEPHANIAH 3:5 | *He knows no injustice*

9/3/97

TAKING THE LOVE in your heart and sharing it with others
makes your love grow.

ISAIAH 66:14 | *Your heart will rejoice.*

7/4/97

TO SEE THE wealthy waste so much is a sorrow, a sorrow that
is afflicted upon those in need. If the wealthy did not
waste but shared in love there would be none in need and
all would be truly wealthy in their hearts.

10/5/97

EACH BREATH, A gift from God.
    Each moment, a gift from God.
    Each person, a gift from God.

Each person should remember that each breath they take
and each moment of their life is a gift from God, a gift
they share with every person.

JEREMIAH 23:24 | *Do I not fill heaven and earth.*

12/9/97

BE GENEROUS IN your giving and expect little in return and you will receive much.

WISDOM 11:7
You gave them abundant water in an un-hoped for way.

9/11/97

THE CROSS CAN be shared by all in their lives if they accept unconditionally My love and understand the cross they carry is a sign of My love and that I carry it with them.

ISAIAH 3:1 | *Support and prop.*

ISAIAH 30:1 | *Who carry.*

25/11/97

GENEROSITY IS A sign of love,
for it is love that makes you generous.

Kindness

15/2/97

KINDNESS STARTS IN your heart,
for when you love you cannot be anything except kind.

ACTS 10:33 | *And you have been kind enough to come.*

1/7/97

BEING KIND SHOULD not be something you force yourself to do but something you want to do.

EZRA 3:5
Voluntary offerings made by individuals to Yahweh.

....

20/8/97

In kindness all are touched,
    in love all are helped and in Me
    all are saved.

2/9/97

TO BE A man...love.
    To be a man...care.
    To be a man...be kind,

Then truly be a man.

PSALMS 62:13
Power belongs to God, so too Lord, does kindness.

1/12/97

BE AWARE OF how your words can hurt others and with this knowledge always speak kindly.

Friendship

5/3/96

FRIENDSHIP, HOPE AND truth. My friendship brings hope to those in search of the truth.

7/3/96

MY FRIENDSHIP IS offered to everyone, it is they who often do not accept it and offer Me their friendship. It is a two-way giving. I give My love and friendship and in return you must give Me yours otherwise it is a one-sided love and a friendship that is ignored. When it is two ways then the exchange of gifts is a wonder to behold; the gifts of love.

ECCLESIASTICUS 22:25
I will not be ashamed to shelter a friend.

15/6/96

SPIRITUAL FRIENDSHIP,
   Spiritual attraction,
   Spiritual love…a gift from God.

15/6/96

FRIENDS OF GOD,
   Friends of man,
   Friends of heaven,

   The Saints.

26/6/96

MY FRIENDSHIP IS for all.
   My love is for all.
   My forgiveness is for all.

All who become My friends find I only have a forgiving
love awaiting them.

....

27/6/96

Friendship lasts through all adversity
otherwise it is not true friendship.

28/6/96

WORDS OF LOVE and friendship win hearts.

11/7/96

LOVE AMONGST FRIENDS is the love all should have as all
   should be friends.

13/7/96

FRIENDSHIP IN GOD is true friendship,
   Friendship in God is love.

15/12/96

GOOD FRIENDS ARE like good wine, with time they get better.

12/1/97

FRIENDSHIP MEANS LOVE otherwise it is not friendship.

11/11/97

TO SHARE YOUR joy with friends is to share your love,
To share your sorrow with friends is to share your love,
To share your life with friends is to share your love.

This is what friends are, for if they truly love you and you
truly love them then they are truly friends.

LAMENTATIONS 5:15 | *The joy of our hearts.*

Creation

16/1/96

WHEN YOU LOOK upon a flower you see its beauty. When
you smell the fragrance of its bouquet you experience its
beauty. When you feel the softness of its petals you touch
its beauty; the beauty of God's creation. Everything is created by God so see God's creative beauty in all things.

GENESIS 1:31
God saw all he had made and indeed it was very good.

3/3/96

WHEN YOU LOOK upon a flower and see its beauty, do you see
the beauty of its creation or just the surface beauty? It is
the same with people. Do you only look at their appear-
ance or do you look at their inner beauty from God?

It is the inner self that is the true gift of creation, not the
physical appearances.

IT IS IN the air,
> It is in your heart,
> It is everywhere.

> It is all around,
> It is there for all,
> It is everywhere.

My love, My forgiveness and My mercy.

A MAN ONE DAY looked at the sky and saw nothing. Another man did the same and saw the beauty of God's creation. One looked with his mind, the other his heart.
What it showed was if you let your mind control your heart you miss so much. If you let your heart control your mind you find so much.

IN THE LOVE of God all was created.
> In the love of God all exist.
> In the love of God all can live forever.

SIRACH 47:13
He built a house in the name of God and established a lasting sanctuary.

TO LOOK UPON another and to see My Father's creation of love is the way to look. When you do this you look from your heart and look in love.

11/11/96

A FLOWER SHOWS THE beauty of God's creation.
  An animal shows the love of God's creation.
  Mankind is the most beautiful expression of
  God's creative love.

  Look to the flowers and see the beauty.
  Look to the animals and see the love.
  Look to mankind and see what you truly
  should be and can be.

1/1/97

NEVER FORGET TO pray each and every day.
  Never forget to love each and every one.
  Never forget to thank God for each and every thing.

  Then you will never forget why God created your being.

  ISAIAH 49:15 | *I will never forget you.*

4/3/97

AS LOVE IS where all of creation came from, then love is what
  all of creation must exist in if it is to survive.

25/3/97

MAN AND WOMAN, created in God's image, an image of love.
  Man and woman, created to live in God's love and to reflect that love.

  Man and woman, created to be different in their func-
  tions on earth but they are the same in spirit.

6/7/97

THE LOVE I have for mankind is the love from which mankind was created; divine love.

JEREMIAH 44:27 | *I am watching over them.*

8/12/97

WHEN YOU ARE in love with Me, you love all of creation and you love all of mankind, for all was created through Me by the Father. So all is part of My love and if you love Me then you must surely love that which is part of My love.

2 CHRONICLES 36:23
All the kingdoms of the earth the Lord, the God of heaven has given to me.

Mankind

16/12/95

FROM THE HEART of God came mankind and to the heart of God must mankind return to find his true home.

22/5/96

A WORK OF LOVE...MANKIND.
A grace from God...life.
A gift of God...redemption.

When mankind can accept that he is created from God's love and that life is a grace from the Father then he will find redemption through Me, God's Son.

12/6/96

MANKIND, CREATED IN love to be love.
    Mankind, created from love to be love.
    Mankind, created with love to be love.

Mankind may have forgotten but God has not.

11/7/96

FLOWERS OF LOVE give off a sweet perfume,
    Flowers of love become a joy to behold.
    Flowers of love brighten the world and fill it with the
    most beautiful fragrance.

All mankind can be flowers of love that grow in the joy of
God to become a beauty to behold.

13/8/96

SINCE MANKIND WAS first created I have loved them.
    For as long as mankind will be, I will love them.
    And in eternity I will want them with Me to share in My
    love.

ECCLESIASTICUS 29:1
*Invest your treasure as the most high orders, and you will
find it more profitable than gold.*

16/11/96

TO UNDERSTAND THE weaknesses of others is an important
    part of understanding yourself, for mankind's weakness-
    es are universal.

JEREMIAH 50:24
You set a snare for yourself and were caught.

18/11/96

A PATH IS PLACED before all of mankind and in the beginning mankind walked on the right path until confused by evil.

I am the right path offered to mankind but often blinded by evil, many cannot see this and many get led to other paths which only lead away from God.

I will be there offering My love to all of mankind in the hope they will return to the true path of God and turn their back on evil so eternal joy in heaven can be theirs.

16/1/97

Showered with love—mankind.
Showered with grace—mankind.
Showered with goodness—mankind.

In love mankind should accept the
grace-filled goodness it is offered.

24/6/97

ALL OVER THE world people are praying
and you hear little of it.
All over the world people are sinning
and you hear of almost nothing else.
All over the world people are lost
and it is plain to see.
All over the world people are searching
and many find Me.

All over the world people live without hope
and many live in despair.
All over the world people reach out
and show they care.

All over the world is good but often the good is hidden by
the bad and a sense of hopelessness fills the air. If people
look for the good they will find it and lift from the world
its despair.

Life

30/11/95

PETER ASKED ONE day, 'Why is it all the people do not love
You when You only come in love?'
I replied, 'If all loved Me then I would not be here, for
there would be no evil to defeat. The reason they do not
love Me is often that they look with their mind, not their
heart, and when they do the things of this world cloud
their sight.'
Today the same is true, if all would think of God's love instead of their needs, their desires, then God's love would
touch all and all would love God.

16/1/96

LIFE IS STRANGE to many they cannot understand why they
are here. They cannot see why life is so difficult at times.
They cannot come to terms with the disasters and wars
in the world. They see so many bad things and cannot be-

lieve in God, for if there is a God He surely would not let these things happen.

What these people do not understand is that God only brings joy, comfort, happiness, goodness and peace to those who want it, it is when you deny God that all the bad things happen. It is when you deny God that life is meaningless. It is when you deny God that life is a burden.

The confused children should see why they are confused and then understand what life really is.

2 PETER 2:12–13
All the same, these people who only insult anything they do not understand are not reasoning beings.

2 PETER 3:14–15
So then my friends while you are waiting do your best to live lives without spot or stain so that he will find you at peace.
Think of our Lord's patience as your opportunity to be saved.

3/12/95

THE WEARY OF heart can find strength in Me, the strength they need for all they do. The tired of spirit can find rest in Me, the rest that renews their soul.

The exhausted of body can find energy in Me, the energy of the Spirit that lifts the weariness from their body.

27/1/96

WHEN YOU STRUGGLE, turn to Me.
When you despair I am there.
When you are lost I will lead you.

Always I am by your side.
Always I am waiting to help.
Always I love you.

1/2/96

MY HAND IS extended to all peoples,
no matter what their belief.

I open My heart to the whole world, no-one is denied.
I offer eternal life to everyone, all are welcome.
I wait for My children to respond and receive what I
offer them.

10/2/96

If you worry over little things
they become big things.

11/2/96

IN LIFE FIND love, for what is life without love?
In love find life for without love what is the point to life?

14/2/96

IN LIFE NOT everything depends on choice but it is by the
choices you make that your life's path is decided. It may
be that one person is born to wealth and another poor.
This is not by chance but it is by God's will.
Whichever you are, rich or poor, you should understand
that it is the choices you make in the rest of your life that
determine your destiny. Being rich can be a millstone just

as being poor can be a burden. It is how you accept your life and then what choices you make within it that can lift the burden or remove the millstone.

If you are rich in heart then you can never be poor but if you are poor in heart then you can never be rich.

26/2/96

AS A FLOWER opens to show its beauty, so opens My heart to show the way.

As the wind blows the trees in the direction it goes, so My Spirit leads God's children in the direction of heaven.

As the water flows in a stream, so flows the mercy of God from My side to wash mankind clean of his sins.

The heart of mankind can be as the flowers, beautiful from within when he accepts the gentle wind of mercy that I offer through My open heart.

1/3/96

WHEN YOU SEE people who have no interest in life or in God you see people sick in the spirit. To help them overcome this pray, pray and pray.

4/3/96

WITH NO DISCIPLINE in life there is no character, for discipline builds character. It is the discipline of love, not violence, of caring, not anger, of help, not rejection, that moulds the character in the true way.

ECCLESIASTICUS 21:11
Whoever keeps the law will master his instincts.

11/3/96

IT IS IN each one's heart to be a good person. It is decided by the free choices each person makes whether or not they become good or evil.

It is the choices for God that make a good person or the choices against God that make a bad person. If a person can see what each choice leads to, then he can understand what he chooses.

To see clearly, look at My Word in Holy Scripture. The choices are clearly described there, you only have to look to find them.

HAGGAI 1:7 | *Reflect carefully how things have gone for you.*

HAGGAI 2:15 | *Reflect carefully from today onwards.*

....

21/6/96

A face of love, the face of God.
A heart of love, the heart of God.

A heart of love that comes face to face
with all at sometime in their life.
For some it is a saving grace while for
others it is a condemnation.

How you live makes the difference.

10/4/96

THE IMPORTANT THING in life is to love, for without love you cannot live.

10/4/96

THE MAZE OF life can only be unraveled with love in your heart. The mystery of life can only be revealed with God in your soul. The majesty of God can only be seen when you live your life in love and fill your soul with the love of God.

23/6/96

LIFE IS A burden without love, for it is in love life was created.

6/7/96

TAKE CARE IN your life, care to recognize how easily evil can lead you down the wrong path.

PSALMS 22:16 | *A pack of dogs surround me.*

10/7/96

ALL PEOPLE ARE offered a guiding hand to walk the path that leads to heaven, yet so many turn away and walk the path that leads to hell.
The choices are so different, one brings happiness forever, the other suffering forever.
Often the differences are covered with confusion, a confusion of evil that is there to take people to the wrong path.
If mankind would look in love from their hearts, remove all pride and be humble, the confusion would disappear and once again the choices would be so clear.

All it takes is for mankind to want heaven and to follow the clear path I laid out before them when I walked this earth.

19/7/96

WALK HAND IN hand with Me and have no fear in life.

19//7/96

SPEND YOUR LIFE loving,
   Spend your life giving,
   Spend your life praising God,

   Then spend eternity in heaven.

5/9/96

TRUTH AND GENTLENESS,
   Kindness and understanding,
   Compassion and forgiveness,

   Live them and give them.

   ISAIAH 51:7
   Listen to me, you who know what integrity means.

6/9/96

BUILD A FOUNDATION in your heart; a foundation of My love. Build a foundation in your soul; a foundation of My spirit. Build a foundation in your life; a foundation of the Sacraments and prayer.

   PSALMS 146:1
   Alleluia! Praise Yahweh my soul. I mean to praise Yahweh all my life.

21/10/96

LOVE IS THE answer to life.
Life is the fruit of love.

Love life for it is a gift of the Father
and in love life is created.

PSALMS 8:50
What is man that God should be mindful of him.

27/10/96

LOVE IS THE essence of life, for if you live without love what
is life. Love is the reason for living, for without love there
is no reason for life. Love is the meaning of life, for without love in your life there is no meaning.

Love God's gift of life, as life is God's gift of love.

COLOSSIANS 1:28 | *The mystery of Christ in you.*

11/11/96

IN A DESERT any oasis looks attractive and often people
would chase after mirages of beautiful oases only to find
they did not exist.
Today the world is like a desert, barren of My love in many
hearts. Often these people chase after illusions that look
as if they bring happiness and the answers to life. How
disappointed they will be when they find in these illusions nothing exists, only pain and suffering.

Before My children rush headlong to an illusion of safety
and security they should look to see what is really offered

to them and they will find unless it is of God it will only bring them sadness and tragedy.

21/12/96

IT IS PRECIOUS, your time on earth so treasure it, enjoy it and do not waste it with worry. Treasure the gift God has given you and enjoy each precious moment.

EZEKIEL 28:26 | *They shall live in confidence.*

23/12/96

The fountain of life is in Me, bathe in My love and you will live forever.

ISAIAH 48:21
Those he led through the deserts never went thirsty.

20/1/97

A SACRAMENTAL LIFE,
A prayerful life,
A loving life,

Lead to God.

2 MACCABEES 2:18
Since he has rescued us from great evils and has purified the temple.

23/3/97

LOVE IS WONDERFUL to live in, for in it life is complete.

PSALMS 103:22 | *Bless the Lord oh my soul.*

25/3/97

TO LOVE IS to live, for without love what is life?

8/5/97

PRAISE GOD IN all you do,
    love God in all you feel,
    live for God in all your life.

9/5/97

PUT LOVE FIRST in your life and then your life becomes love.

JEREMIAH 50:5 | *Let us bind ourselves to Yahweh.*

12/5/97

TO LOVE IS to live, for what is life without love?
    To love is to be complete in Me, for I am love and when
    you truly love then you know Me.

13/5/97

A PLEASURE IN LIFE can be a chain in eternity
    if it is a pleasure of sin.
    A pleasure in life can be a gift of eternal joy
    if it is the pleasure of doing God's will.

    A pleasure in life can only truly be a pleasure
    if it is of God's eternal love and for God's eternal joy.

14/5/97

PRECIOUS MOMENTS, MOMENTS of life.
Precious life, each moment.
Precious gift, the gift of each moment of life.

27/6/97

PLACING THE EUCHARIST in the centre of your life brings true life and true peace.

HOSEA 10:1 | *Yielding plenty of fruit.*

....

1/7/97

Precious to Me is each soul.
Precious to Me is each person.
Precious to Me is each life.

Each should be precious to man also.

EZEKIEL 37:27
I will be their God and they shall be my people.

7/8/97

LOVE IS THE key to life.
Love is the answer to life.
Love is the reason for life, for love is life.

MICAH 1:2 | *And all that fills you.*

4/9/97

IT IS A time when the world needs to change its outlook on life, a time to see the true value of life and a time to appreciate life for the gift it is, a gift of God's love.

When the world once again values life it once again will start to love and it will once again find peace.

JOHN 7:6 | *The time is always right.*

....

8/11/97

Love, the key to life, for without love,
what life is there and what value is
life?

JEREMIAH 22:13
Woe to him who builds his house on wrong.

17/11/97

TREAT EACH PERSON in the way you would like to be treated yourself and then find you treat them as you should.

28/11/97

LOVE IS THE reason for living and when you discover this then you can start to live.

PSALMS 136:1 | *God's love endures forever.*

29/11/97

IN A LIFE without love there is pain and despair.
In a life without love comes hatred and anger.
In a life without love enters sin and evil.

Always love everyone and give them the chance to feel
wanted and to feel they are important, then you give
them the chance to let love into their lives once more.

PROVERBS 3:27 | *Refuse no one.*

13/12/97

IT IS THE way of the world today to take advantage of others, to put yourself and your needs first and to ignore the
plight of those in need. This is the way of the world but
not the way of God.
If people remain in the world's way they close their hearts
to the true way of life and embrace what will lead them to
pay a price they will wish they did not have to.

Embrace the true way and live. I am the way, the only way
that leads to heaven.

JOHN 15:18
If the world hates you realize it hated me first.

Death

IN DEATH FIND life.
>   In death see happiness.
>   In death find the gift of God's love.

DEATH, AS LIFE, can be a joy or can be a misery.
>   Death and life the same, inseparable.

>   If both are in God's love they become a joy, if not, a misery.

OPENING THE DOOR to heaven means closing the door to life on earth. There is no other way for mankind; so understand what waits behind the door is glorious and what you leave behind is but a moment.

....

When a child comes home there are
celebrations and so it is in heaven
each time a soul returns to God.

4/1/96

DURING LIFE SEE with eyes of love
and in death find the rewards.

2/5/96

IN DEATH SEE life.
In death welcome heaven.
In death awaken to love.

I am love which leads you to life eternal in heaven and in
Me find the truth of death.

16/6/96

DEATH, A DOOR to heaven. Death, a step to God. Death, a walk
to eternity.
In life if you have lived in God the rewards are found
in death. In life you walk the path that can lead you to
heaven for eternity. In life each step should be a step for
God then in death you will find eternal peace in heaven.

6/7/96

IN DEATH, FIND joy.
In death, find life.
In death, find God.

22/1/97

DEATH IS A gift. Death is the beginning of eternity in My
love for those who believe in Me.
Death is there for all and all should see it for what it is:
God's gift that can bring you to eternal love in Me if you
believe.

JOEL 3:23 | *Rejoice in Yahweh your God.*

30/3/97

WHY FEAR DEATH when it can bring true life.
Only fear sin, for it is this that can bring true death.

PSALMS 78:65–66
The Lord woke up to strike his enemies on the rump and re-
turn them to everlasting shame.

5/7/97

THE LOSS OF a loved one in death is truly not a loss just a
parting for a while. In eternity you meet again and in love
you can exist forever if you trust and believe in Me.

1 MACCABEES 7:48
The people rejoiced greatly and observed that day as a great
festival.

1/9/97

GRIEF IS RELIEVED by sharing.
Grief is relieved by caring.
Grief is relieved by baring.

When you bare your soul and share your feelings of grief
you show how much you cared for the dead and give others the opportunity to care for you.

EZEKIEL 17:24 | *And make the withered tree bloom.*

6/9/97

SADNESS AND SORROW in a death.
Joy and hope in a death.
Glory and praise in a death.

It is with sadness that most see death, as most are filled with sorrow at the loss of a loved one.
In death, however, is the hope of eternal joy for those who come to the glory of God in heaven and sing His praises eternally.

MATTHEW 26:6
From now on you will see the son of man seated at the right hand of the power.

....

6/9/97

Imagine nothing after death,
        then imagine life without hope
        and life without meaning.

EZEKIEL 23:33 | *A cup of dismay.*

15/9/97

HAPPINESS IN DEATH is a gift of life.

SIRACH 24:19
You will remember me as sweeter than honey.

Resurrection

30/3/97

I HAVE RISEN FROM the dead to show the world life after death does exist. With My rising I say to mankind, follow Me and come to glory in heaven.

JEREMIAH 50:44 | *Name me the shepherd.*

The Gift of a Body

19/8/96

MY HEART WEEPS at the promiscuity in the world. Mankind has, it seems, forgotten what a gift they have from God in their bodies.

Bodies which are created to be temples of God's love. Bodies which are there to be respected. Bodies which deserve to be cared for and treated with the value they have.

How sad it is when God's gift is thought of as mankind's to do with as he wants, to use only for self or for pleasure.

What a waste of a gift and what a rejection of God.

1/10/96

BODIES ARE A gift from God and should be respected. So often bodies are seen as instruments of pleasure there to be abused with drugs or bad living.

A gift from God should be treasured and cared for, then the gift can become what it was given for.
Bodies were given so that man may grow in God's love and come to live eternally in heaven.
Mankind should understand this and treat their bodies with respect and in the way they deserve.

19/12/96

THE LOVE OF your body can be a sin if it is loved above all else.
The love of your body should be the love of God's creation and the gift He gives to you.
The love of your body needs to be the love of the miracle of God's love within you.

ISAIAH 66:22 | *So will your race and name endure.*

22/10/97

IN SICKNESS REST is important for without it recovery is more difficult. In sickness sacrifices are made by offering the pain to Me but I do not expect people to place themselves in situations where the sickness will get worse. In sickness you have a choice to care for your body so it will recover and can continue to do My work, or a choice to ignore your body and maybe make your illness worse, preventing you from doing My will.
Your body is a gift of God so you should treat it as such and understand if I ask for a sacrifice I will place the cross upon you. All you need to do is embrace it, not try to make it heavier.

2 CORINTHIANS 6:3 | *Cause no one to stumble.*

Families

2/12/95

FAMILIES BECOME UNITED in love and parted in sin.

17/12/95

WHEN YOUR FAMILY takes all you have to give and expects to give nothing in return and when they abuse you when you ask for what is due then you know some of the pain I feel each time a child of God treats Me so.

4/2/96

IT IS NORMAL for families sometimes to have difficult moments but the strength of the family is shown in how it overcomes those moments.

8/3/96

FAMILIES ARE CREATED in love to be love.
Families are created to be united with each other.
Families are created to bring peace to the world.

Without families sin reigns.
Without families evil abounds.
Without families there is no love.

Families, so important to God and to mankind.
Families, so strong when they unite.
Families, so much love to share.

8/4/96

FRIENDS IN CHRIST.
Brothers and sisters in Christ.
Family in Christ.

All those who love Me.

17/4/96

LOVE OF ONE'S family should be the love you have for all.
Help to one's family should be the help for all. Sharing
with one's family should be a sharing with all.

All are your family so treat them as such.

5/5/96

FAMILIES, FULL OF love, a joy.
Families, full of hate, a burden.
Families, full of giving, glorious.
Families, full of self, a scandal.

6/5/96

IN SICKNESS, IN health, in poverty, in wealth.
All are your family and all need help.

10/5/96

AS A FAMILY loves each other the family grows and grows.
As a family cares for each other the family is strengthened.

As a family, mankind needs to love and care for each
other so that it can find the strength to grow as it was
created to.

7/9/96

IN A FAMILY love can flourish if it is nurtured.
In a family love can die if it is ignored.
In a family love can be a family's strength.
In a family love can be a family's weakness.

In a family love can mean so much.
In a family love can mean so little.
In a family love embraced is a choice in which a family can flourish, be strengthened and mean so much to each other.
In a family love ignored is a choice which weakens the family that does not nurture it.

Love, the mainstay of family life.
I am love and I am there for all families.

ECCLESIASTICUS 40:15
The offshoots of the Godless will not have many branches, unclean roots only find hard rock.

14/9/96

A FAMILY OF LOVE, My love.
A family of hope, My hope.
A family of truth, My truth.

In those who follow Me see the truth that joins all in love to become one family filled with hope for the future.

25/12/96

A FAMILY MAY HAVE problems but it is still a family and in love all its problems can be overcome.

9/7/97

TREAT ALL MEN as brothers, all women as sisters then all mankind becomes for you what it truly is, your family.

ISAIAH 7:17 | *You and your people.*

12/7/97

A FAMILY CAN ONLY be complete when there is love.
A family can only be united when there is love.
A family can only be a family when there is love.

I am love and I should be at the centre of each family to make it complete and united with God.

BARUCH 3:13
Had you walked in the way of God you would have dwelt in enduring peace.

Marriage

3/6/96

JOINED IN LOVE, husband and wife.
Joined in God, husband wife.
Joined for eternity, husband and wife.

A special grace within the wonderful gift of marriage.

14/7/96

A WIFE, PART OF her husband. A husband, part of his wife.
Together joined by love in Me.

15/2/97

HUSBAND AND WIFE should be together for life. Husband and wife should be joined in God in their daily life. Husband and wife should be certain that in God's love for them is eternal life.

Marriage is a gift of God that if lived as a gift of love becomes a reflection of God's graces to mankind.

ACTS 20:19 | *Serving the Lord with all humility.*

....

2/5/97

Love between a husband and wife is a
gift from God, remember that always
and treasure it.

10/7/97

A HUSBAND AND WIFE must be united in love
for a marriage to survive.
A husband and wife must be joined by trust
for a marriage to survive.
A husband and wife must be one in God
for a marriage to survive.

Without these how can it be called a true marriage and how can it survive. Without these it is a marriage in name only.

21/9/97

UNITED IN LOVE, marriage.
United for life, marriage.
United in a promise to God to love each other for life.

That is the truth of marriage which is so often forgotten.

PSALMS 81:5 | *An edict of the God of Jacob.*

Children of God

5/1/96

INSIDE EVERY PERSON is a little child who wants to be loved
and cared about.
If each one could look to this child and set it free they
could become what they were made to be, innocent and
pure.

The love they need is there for them and if they become
childlike again the love of God will care for and protect
them.

5/3/96

ALL MY CHILDREN are loved by Me but
do all My children love Me?
All My children are wanted by Me but
do all My children want Me?
All My children are forgiven by Me but
do all My children ask for My forgiveness?

28/6/96

IT IS A joy to My heart when I see how strong men become
as children when they find My love.
It is a sadness to My heart when I see how strong men
become evil when they lose My love.
It is a grace from My heart that the wicked can be forgiven and become as little children again.

24/1/97

What fathers do for their children
is a sign of their love.

What I did for My children is love.

SONG OF SONGS 8:7
Love, no flood can quench.

26/1/97

CHILDREN TODAY ARE surrounded by confusion, no wonder
they stray. Children today are surrounded by sin, no wonder they do the same. Children today are surrounded by
hate, no wonder they find it hard to love.

Today's children need what children have always needed,
love, caring and guidance. Parents today must offer this
in Me and not in themselves.

ECCLESIASTICUS 11:20
Persevere at your duty, take pleasure in doing it.

14/7/97

CHILDREN BECOME ADULTS too soon and today childhood
seems to be lost. Without childhood people become hard
and unloving.

Let the children be children and let their lives be whole.

HAGGAI 1:7 | *Consider your ways.*

26/8/97

LOVE IS THE gift of God's joy.
Love is the reward of God's children.
Love is the way of God.

I am the way, for I am God and I offer the gift of My love
to all My children.

EZEKIEL 22:1 | *The Lord came to Me.*

26/8/97

CHILDREN FILLED WITH innocent love
show how all should be.

ISAIAH 65:14 | *For joy of heart.*

8/10/97

INSIDE EACH PERSON is a little child searching for love, a
child searching for hope and a child searching for security; inside My heart they will find all of these and more
than they could have ever imagined.

21/11/97

MANY TIMES PARENTS worry over their children. It begins when the child is born and only ends when death greets the parents or their child.

The worry is the concern of love and the love is a gift of God just as life is. Knowing this, parents should trust that God will look after their children and truly there is nothing to worry about if they do so.

EPHESIANS 6:4
Bring them up with the training and instruction of the Lord.

28/11/97

BECOME AS A child, innocent in My love.
Become as a child, trusting in My love.
Become as a child, taking My hand and walking in My love.

SIRACH 39:13 | *My faithful children.*

12/12/97

CONSIDER THE LOVE of a baby then be like that.

The Young

16/9/96

YOUNG PEOPLE...THE CHURCH of the future. Young people... the hope of the future. Young people...the life of the future. In the young is the hope that tomorrow will bring true life filled with My love.

Choice

3/6/96

IN A HEART there can be love or there can be hate.
In a soul there can be light or dark.
In a thought there can be good or bad.

There is always a choice in everything you do. Make the right choice and have your heart filled with goodness so that your soul will come to heaven to live in the light of My love forever.

ISAIAH 49:10 | *They will never hunger or thirst.*

12/12/96

THERE IS A time in everyone's life when they have a decision to make. They decide to follow the path of God or to ignore it.
Those who choose for God choose eternal joy. Those who choose to ignore God choose a path that may lead to eternal suffering.

Choose God and choose eternal life.
Choose evil and choose eternal suffering.

JEREMIAH 23:20 | *The decision of his heart.*

17/6/97

Before each person are two choices,
the choices of accepting God or denying God. They are not choices you
make only once but make over and
over in each moment that is your life.

24/7/97

WITH GOD IN your life you live.
With sin in your life you die.
With love in your life you are happy.
With hate in your life you are sad.

With hope in your life you have a reason to live.
With evil in your life you have no reason at all.
With God's love in your life hope springs eternal
and gives your life a meaning.
With evil in your life the sins you live bring a sadness
that gives life no meaning.

With the right choice, the choice of God, you will exist in
happiness forever. Choose wisely.

EZEKIEL 14:6 | *Return and be converted from your idols.*

7/8/97

A MAN CAN BE a sign of humble love and
a joy to all he meets or a man can be a sign of pride and a
misery to those he meets.

Choose humility and be a joy,
choose pride and be lost.

18/10/97

A MAN MAY FACE many choices in his life. With each choice it is important to take the time to weigh the disadvantages against the advantages. With proper consideration the correct choice becomes clearer and the wrong choice obvious.

Even so, many still make the wrong choices because what may appear to be wrong can often be made to look acceptable with excuses and deceptions. Often the wrong choice can seem the most attractive, so it is important when making decisions in your life to ask for My guidance and if you do I will help you make the best choices in your life.

I am waiting to help everyone make the right choices so that their lives can be happy ones by choosing the right path to walk on earth which will lead to heaven in eternity.

If you ask I will help and if you choose to accept My help heaven will be yours.

27/10/97

LIFE CAN BE a cross of joy or a cross of sadness. The choice is each person's.

With the certainty that each person will carry a cross in life they should decide how they want to carry it and how their life will be.

A cross of joy is one carried for God and brings eternal rewards. A cross of sadness is one carried in self and brings eternal suffering.

LUKE 14:27
Whoever does not carry his own cross and come after me cannot be my disciple.

Happiness and Joy

31/12/95

BE HAPPY IN My love.
> Be joyful in My love.
> Be one with Me in My love.

14/1/96

SING THE JOYS of God's salvation.
> Sing the joys of God's love.
> Sing the joys of God's glorious victory.

> Sing the joys of God's Son.
> Sing the joys of God's mercy.
> Sing the joys of God's forgiveness.

> PSALMS 89:1 | *I will celebrate your love forever Yahweh.*

16/1/96

HAPPINESS COMES FROM love,
> Joy comes from love,
> Peace comes from love,

> I am love and I bring these.

10/2/96

THE JOY OF being in love with Me is a joy for all people.
> The joy of being in My service is a joy for all people.
> The joy of being at one with Me is a joy for all people...
> The joy that is the love of God.

HAPPINESS IS A grace from God.
   Love is a gift from God.

   The love of God is given gracefully
   as a gift that brings happiness.

VOICES RAISED IN song often lose the joy that should come
   with this gift. Sometimes the songs are songs of evil and
   sin, then the voices become voices of anger and hate.
   Sometimes the songs are of false love, then the voices
   become voices of seduction, seduction into sin and are
   disguised from what they really are, evil.
   Other songs sing the praises of God, the love of God and
   each other. These are the songs that lift the hearts in joy
   and show what a gift song can be, a gift from God.

....

It brings joy... My love.
      It brings life...My love.
      It brings eternity...My love.

      My love brings joy to life
      and brings life to eternity.

THE JOY IN your heart is My love.
   The love in your heart is My joy.

26/7/96

THE JOY IN the voice of one whom loves God
is a beacon to those who do not.

10/8/96

EXCITEMENT IN MY love,
Joy in My love,
Happiness in My love,

There for all but few accept it.

28/9/96

IT IS WITH joy I look upon those who love Me,
a joy I long to share with all My children.
It is with love I look upon those who find joy in Me,
a love I long to share with all My children.

It is the joy of loving Me and, through Me, My Father and the Holy Spirit, that awaits all who come to heaven; an eternal joy that is there for all who truly seek it.

PSALMS 49:1
Hear this all nations, pay attention all who live on earth.

27/12/96

IN JOY LIVE, in joy love, in joy live your life and in joy give your love and then find joy with Me in eternity.

EZEKIEL 20:40
There I will welcome you and there expect your presents.

1/1/97

THE EXCITEMENT OF love, the joy of love,
the happiness of love...

Wonderful gifts of God.

HABAKKUK 1:16
Providing them with luxury and lavish food.

....

4/4/97

See the joy of the love of one
who cares for you, then see it is
a reflection of My love.

3/5/97

MY JOY IS complete when mankind returns to Me and accepts My love.

ISAIAH 66:5 | *Let us witness your joy.*

13/5/97

IN LOVE LIFE is a joy,
In love each person is a joy,
In love every moment is a joy.

It is in love you see people for what they truly are, a creation of God's joyful love from which life springs eternal, and each moment becomes a joy of God's gift of life.

14/5/97

MY LOVE, A love for all.
My joy, a joy for all.
My heart, a heart for all.

If all would love Me they would find that the joy of being in My heart fulfils their life.

....

25/6/97

When you see love it makes you happy for this is what love brings, happiness!

8/7/97

HUMOUR IS A gift, a gift that should bring joy to all and offend no one.

8/7/97

MORE FAITH, MORE trust and more love are what mankind needs if it is to reach eternal joy.

BARUCH 4:24 | *So shall they soon see God's salvation.*

12/7/97

PLEASURE IS ONLY truly pleasure when it is pleasure in Me and in My commandments.

PROVERBS 3:18 | *And he is happy who holds her fast.*

24/7/97

WHEN LOVE FILLS you happiness follows.
When love fills you joy is in your heart.
When love fills you God is with you.

EZEKIEL 24:32 | *Which holds so much.*

....

2/11/97

Never be jealous of others instead be
happy for their achievements espe-
cially if they are achieved in Me.

EPHESIANS 5:4 | *But instead thanksgiving.*

12/11/97

LOVE IS THE joy of life, for without love how can there be joy
in your life.

JOB 21:18 | *Though his wealth increases he shall not rejoice.*

Confusion

31/7/96

IT IS WITH sadness I look into the hearts of My confused children. I look and see how easily they are led from Me, how
easily they commit sin and think nothing of it, how easily

self comes first. Confusion reigns supreme in many but often they do not see it.

To lift this cloud they only need to ask for My help. Ask and they will receive. Ask and make Me happy.

2/8/96

CONFUSION IS ALWAYS cleared by the truth. I am the truth.

Clarity

9/6/96

TO SEE THE world as it is takes a clear mind, a clear heart and a clear soul. A clear mind that sees in love, a clear heart that feels with love, and a clear spirit full of love.

30/7/96

WHEN YOUR THOUGHTS wander, think of Me. When your mind is distracted, think of Me. When your heart is confused, think of Me.

Thinking of Me clears the confusion, removes the distraction and brings you to the path you may be wandering from.

12/9/97

CLARITY COMES WITH prayer,
Clarity comes through the Sacraments,

Clarity comes in Me.

PSALMS 36:21 | *Our eyes relish the sight.*

Truly Seeing

7/1/96

TO SEE SPIRITUALLY you need to open your heart in love.
When you love God completely your spirit becomes aware
of God's love in all things.
You become aware of God's love everywhere and you become aware you are God's, this is spiritual sight.

14/4/96

Eyes of love look from the heart and
see into the heart.

27/6/96

SEE IN EACH person My love, even if it is hidden in most
it is still there. Through prayer, love and kindness help
them release My love into their hearts then see the world
change.

27/12/96

IN THE EYE is the gift of vision.
In the soul is the gift of spiritual sight.

In the world both can become blinded
but in love both can be healed.

27/12/96

TO SEE IN others the love of God is to look in the way I ask.

ECCLESIASTICUS 35:8 | *Add a smiling face to all your gifts.*

17/2/97

LOOKING FOR DISASTER brings disaster,
Looking in hope brings rewards.

2 CHRONICLES 26:5 | *Set himself to seek God.*

25/8/97

IN SIN MANY are blinded but if they turn to Me they will see.

EZEKIEL 14:8 | *Thus you shall know that I am the Lord.*

1/9/97

LOOK TO THE future in Me.
Look to the past in Me.
Look to the present in Me.

Then you see the world as you should, in My eyes.

LAMENTATIONS 3:3 | *Again and again all the day.*

20/10/97

IN EACH PERSON see My love.
In each person see My gift.
In each person see My grace.

Then in each person you see what you should.

LUKE 14:33 | *Everyone of you.*

28/10/97

WHEN YOU SHOW love to others you show love to Me.
When you ignore others you ignore Me.

When you look upon others see Me and treat them
as you would treat Me; treat them with love.

PSALMS 141:5 | *That is kindness.*

2/11/97

THROUGH MY EYES you will see only with love.
Through My eyes you will see only with caring.
Through My eyes you will see only with forgiveness.

Everyone should try to look through My eyes.

PSALMS 68:4 | *They will celebrate with great joy.*

9/12/97

WHEN YOU SEE another see them with eyes of love and eyes
of hope that in their heart My love still burns.

Wisdom

26/6/96

WISDOM COMES FROM understanding and
accepting God's will in your life.

Any other wisdom is a false wisdom.

17/6/97

THE WISEST MAN knows nothing unless he knows Me.

JOHN 8:24 | *Unless you come to believe that I Am.*

17/8/97

WISDOM COMES FROM learning from your mistakes and from seeing your weaknesses and coming to terms with them by My grace.

HOSEA 5:15 | *And seek my presence.*

19/8/97

THE WISE ARE those who are obedient to My will. The foolish are those who are obedient only to themselves. The wise are humble, the foolish proud.

Wisdom brings you to heaven but foolishness only brings you to pain. Be wise!

JEREMIAH 5:31 | *Yet my people will have it so.*

....

2/12/97

It is wise to love; folly to hate.

JEREMIAH 46:11 | *No use to.*

Denial

17/1/97

NEVER DENY ANYONE help,
>   Never deny anyone prayers,
>   Never deny anyone love,

>   For if you do then you deny Me.

>   PSALMS 78:37 | *In their hearts they were not true to him.*

6/7/97

NEVER BREAK THE commandments.
>   Never commit sin.
>   Never deny God,
>   and you will never be overcome.

>   JOHN 12:50 | *And I know his commandment is eternal life.*

The Poor

1/11/96

REMEMBER THE POOR:
>   The poor of heart need love. The poor of spirit need God.
>   The poor of the world need feeding. My love is the food of
>   God which feeds the poor and heals their hearts and souls.

14/1/97

THE GENEROSITY OF the poor makes the rich the true poor.

8/9/97

THE POOR ARE always in need because the rich ignore them.

SONGS 3:2 | *Whom my heart loves.*

6/11/97

MONEY OFTEN BLINDS people to life, for when people make
money their god, their life becomes truly empty and they
become the poor of the world.

WISDOM 12:2
Warn them and remind them of the sins they are committing.

Need

12/6/96

ENCOURAGEMENT IS NEEDED by all, with encouragement
people grow and are strengthened.

1/9/96

FIND IN ME all you need to live,
 Find in Me all you need to love,
 Find in Me all you need to live eternally in love.

HOSEA 12:6
Hold fast to love and justice and always put trust in your God.

16/3/97

WHAT YOU EXPECT is not always what you receive but what you receive is always what you need.

MATTHEW 13:22–23
And anyone who received the seed in rich soil is the man who hears the word and understands it; he is the one who yields a harvest and produces now a hundred fold.

15/4/97

PRAISE THOSE WHO love Me, love those who praise Me and give to those who need Me.

2/12/97

WHEN DISASTERS STRIKE in the world mankind needs to unite and respond in love to those in need. If they do not then this is the true disaster.

SIRACH 2:7 | *Turn not away.*

Suffering

16/1/96

IN THE PAIN that most feel within at sometime in their life is a saving grace that can strengthen and deepen the spiritual understanding of life,
if in the times of painful experiences people see the peace and comfort I gave to all as I carried their hurt on the cross and overcame it.

16/2/96

IT HURTS WHEN you are rejected by those you love.
 It hurts when they show you contempt.
 It hurts when they show you hate.
 It hurts because you love them so much.

 If you didn't it wouldn't hurt.

 ISAIAH 51:7
 Do not fear the taunts of men nor be dismayed by their insults.

26/2/96

A CROSS CAN BE a joy or a sorrow.
 If you look at your cross
 as sharing in My love then it can be a joy.
 If you look at your cross
 in self pity then it can be a sorrow.

11/3/96

IN SICKNESS SEE strength, a strength to keep loving.
 In sickness see faith, the faith you have in Me.
 In sickness see faithful love that gives you the strength
 to overcome in Me.

 JOHN 15:7 | *If you remain in me.*

14/6/96

MY LOVE LIFTS the sadness in life and replaces it with joy.
 My heart takes the pain of life and replaces it with peace.
 My Spirit touches souls and fills them with graces.

 I offer so much and ask so little but so few want what I
 offer.

MY HAND REACHES out to those in need.
    My heart is opened to those in pain.
    My Spirit offers peace to those who are troubled.

Turn to Me for all you need, find your troubles eased and
your pain comforted.

JEREMIAH 31:3 | *I have loved you with an everlasting love.*

WHEN YOU UNITE in My love you unite in My suffering, for
    My suffering is because of the love I have for mankind.

2 CORINTHIANS *1:8*
*So I am asking you to give some definite proof of your love
for him.*

IN PAIN FIND joy when you offer it to Me as a gift of love.

ISAIAH 57:19 | *'I will indeed heal him,' says Yahweh.*

WITHOUT LOVE IN your life there is only pain.
    Without love in your life there is only suffering.
    Without love in your life there is only an empty heart.

EPHESIANS 5:2 | *Live in love.*

1 CORINTHIANS *1:3* | *And peace from God our Father.*

ISAIAH 9:6 | *Both now and forever.*

Healing

4/7/97

THE HEALING I offer is for all people and all sicknesses.
The healing I give is the true healing.

The healing I shower upon those who ask is the eternal healing of love.

LUKE 16:9 | *You will be welcomed into eternal dwellings.*

Sacrifices

29/7/97

SACRIFICES ARE A way of growing in grace.
Sacrifices are a way of declaring your love.
Sacrifices are always rewarded as I grace you in My love.

MARK 13:13
The one who perseveres to the end will be saved.

Hope

23/3/96

WITH HOPE ALL live their lives. Hoping for love, hoping for help, hoping for understanding, hoping for sharing, hoping for freedom, hoping for truth and hoping for forgiveness.

If only all would look to Me their hopes would be found.

BARUCH 4:21 | *Take courage my children call on God.*

14/5/96

CASTING A LINE into the water the fisherman hopes his catch will be good. Sometimes he catches nothing and other times he catches a lot but he always returns in the hope of a big catch.
As a fisher of men My followers must always keep this hope and you will find many big catches.
Know that one soul is a wonderful catch and for each soul saved there awaits a big reward.

13/8/96

LOVE AND HOPE are found in Me, for I am love and I am the only hope for mankind.

Blessings

BLESSINGS ABOUND FOR those who love. Blessings abound for those who care. Blessings abound for those who know I am there.

PSALMS 88:9 | *Yahweh I invoke you all day.*

....

It is a joy to receive a blessing.
It is a grace to receive such a gift.

It is a gift you can only receive from a priest in My name, the blessing of God.

ACTS 10:38 | *How God anointed.*

Humility

11/4/96

HUMILITY IS FOUND with love,
for with true love how can you not be humble.

24/5/96

HUMILITY MEANS GIVING of self completely for others.
Humility means accepting God's will completely
in your life.
Humility means only thinking of how to give for God and
in God's will.

10/7/96

HUMILITY COMES WITH love of God, for when you love God
you see how great is God, how great is His mercy and you
see how you truly are.

29/7/96

HUMILITY STRENGTHENS YOUR heart, deepens your faith
and sweetens your spirit. Be humble.

27/1/97

REMEMBERING YOUR FAULTS helps you understand the
faults of others.

PROVERBS 22:17
Give ear to my words and apply your heart to knowing them.

Evil

9/6/96

EVIL DESTROYS,
  Love builds.

  Evil confuses,
  Love clarifies.

  Evil causes pain and suffering,
  Love brings joy and comfort.

  Evil breaks hearts,
  Love mends hearts.

  Evil desecrates,
  Love consecrates.

  Evil cannot win,
  Love cannot lose.

  Evil, already defeated,
  Love, already overcame.

30/6/96

THERE IS LOVE in the world but often it is hidden.
  There is joy in the world but who hears of it?
  There is hope in the world but who knows about it?
  The silence is deafening where there is good but
  the noise is overwhelming where there is evil.

Evil, made to look exciting. Good, made to seem boring.
What a deception.

JOHN 4:13
Whoever drinks this water will get thirsty again; but anyone
who drinks the water I shall give will never thirst again.

1/1/97

The answer to overcoming sin is love.
The answer to defeating evil is love.
The answer to the salvation of man-
kind is love.

I am love.

ECCLESIASTICUS 39:23
No one can diminish his power to save.

9/2/97

ISN'T IT STRANGE how evil often is preferred over good.
How, even when the results of embracing evil are seen,
many find it hard to let go of it. Evil seems to be accepted
and welcomed by many when it should be rejected and
shunned by all.

Evil, a way of life today, when really it is the way of death.

ISAIAH 55:7
Let them return to the Lord that he may have mercy on them.

9/3/97

SEE THE CONFUSION, the suffering and the pain evil causes
then overcome it in love.

PSALMS 107:8 | *Thank Yahweh for his love.*

26/7/97

OPPRESSION RULES WHEREVER there is inequality.
Oppression rules wherever there is greed.
Oppression rules wherever there is no love of God.

ISAIAH 1:4 | *Ah sinful nation, people laden with wickedness.*

11/10/97

WHEN AN EVIL is removed from a country, unless it is replaced
by goodness, another evil will take its place. In Russia one
evil was defeated but goodness was not embraced and so
evil returned.
The prayers for Russia today are the same as when it was
under the yoke of communism. Russia needs prayers for
its conversion and prayers that the hearts of the people
will embrace goodness.

Today Russia calls out for prayers. Answer that call and
help peace reign in this great land.

LUKE 1:21 | *Meanwhile the people were waiting.*

21/10/97

THE POWER OF My love overcomes all evil so to overcome
evil in your life live in My love.

NAHUM 1:3 | *Great in power.*

Sin

26/3/96

THE PAIN GOES deep into My heart with each sin that is committed. Each sin tears at My soul and each sin reminds Me of how weak is man and how much help he needs. I offer this help on the cross, I offer this help through My mercy and I offer this help to all.

28/5/96

MAKE ALLOWANCES FOR humanity but never accept sin. The acceptance of sin is never allowed no matter what the reason, no matter what the excuse.

12/6/96

AS A RIVER flows towards the sea to become one in the ocean, so it is with the souls of mankind; they flow towards God to become one in eternity. As with a river that is diverted or blocked and does not reach the sea, so it is with man when he is diverted by sin or blocked by the acceptance of evil, then he may not reach God in eternity.

29/1/97

THE BLOOD I shed for mankind washed the stain of sin from many souls. Unfortunately there are those who avoid My forgiving love and bathe over and over in the darkness of sin. I forgive those who ask, I feel sad for those who do not ask and I love all whoever they are.

PSALMS 17:2 | *From your presence my sentence will come.*

A FISH THAT SWIMS against the current eventually tires and is defeated. Sin is like this, eventually it will become tired for it does not have the strength to survive, then it will accept it has been defeated by the current of love that flowed from My side.

1 MACCABEES 3:9
His name resounds to the end of the earth.

OLDER PEOPLE SHOULD be shown respect but you should never accept what is wrong in what they say, do, or suggest. Age is no excuse to accept sin.

GLUTTONY IS A sin that many commit but do not see. So many eat more than they need and continue to do so while others starve. So many eat and eat then become overweight and unhealthy. Many then spend money to lose the excess weight they should have never put on in the first place. What a waste! Buying and eating too much food, then paying to lose it. Such a subtle sin that many cannot see but for each mouth of excess food there is a mouth without food. This is a sin.

EZEKIEL 18:30 | *Is it not what you do that is unjust.*

TO BE HAPPY over other people's weaknesses is a sin. To be sad, a grace, and to be forgiving, a gift.

PROVERBS 18:20 | *Walk in the way of virtue.*

27/8/97

DO NOT BE vengeful.
Do not be resentful.
Do not be unforgiving or you will sin.

7/9/97

LIES ARE EVERYWHERE and today so often they are not hidden, they only try to be justified.

EPHESIANS 5:15 | *Watch carefully then how you live.*

12/12/97

TO MAKE DERISORY comments about others harms the one who makes the comments, for by his words he sins and hurts his very soul.

MARK 9:22 | *Have compassion*

Pride and Selfishness

2/2/96

GOOD PEOPLE BLINDED by pride become
what they hope not to be.

6/2/96

AS I WATCHED two men arguing one day over God's words and God's will I wondered how they did not see that neither of them was living to God's will. How could they be? There was anger, hatred, disdain and pride in their argument and these are not of God.

These two men are like many today in their fervour to love God; they actually close their hearts to God and deceive themselves into believing that they are loyal servants who know best.

....

24/3/96

Strength is found in humility
not in pride.

23/4/96

TO GLORIFY GOD be humble. To glorify God be kind.
To glorify God be love.

20/6/96

WITH HUMILITY YOU grow,
With pride you wither...be humble.

23/6/96

IT IS WITH love I open My heart to all.
It is with pride many reject Me.
It is in love I offer My forgiveness to all.
It is with pride many reject it.
It is for love I gave My life as an offering to
the Father for the forgiveness of sin.
It is in pride many reject it and it is in pride
many will be lost.

PSALMS 38:11
My friends and companions shrink from my wounds

30/8/96

A DARKNESS COVERS MANY hearts and stops My love for entering them. The darkness is called pride. The darkness is of self. The darkness is a barrier to My love.

Lift this darkness in prayer, in the Sacraments and in love. Lift this darkness and live.

JOHN 12:43
They preferred to be approved by people than by God.

JOEL 3:5 | *All who call on the name of Yahweh will be saved.*

4/3/97

PRESTIGE MEANS LITTLE,
Pride means nothing,
Personal gain means even less when you love Me.

27/6/97

IN HUMANITY IS a deep pride that often rules lives. To overcome this pride you first need to recognize it and then face it. Once you are doing this you start to defeat your pride. Once you recognize it is by God's grace you exist, your pride can become your humility.

JONAH 2:8–9 | *I remembered Yahweh.*

27/6/97

DO NOT CONDEMN others for what you would do yourself.

19/7/97

PRIDE DWELLS IN every man but also within every man is the power to overcome it—the power of My love.

5/10/97

TO IMPOSE UPON others without considering their needs is
selfish no matter what the reason.

Greed

2/10/96

GREED CLOSES HEARTS to God;
    generosity opens them.

26/10/97

ONLY SEEK WHAT you need in this life,
    to seek anymore is greed.

Offering

16/3/96

MY HANDS ARE offered to all people, offered as a helping,
steadying influence to assist them in walking the path to
heaven.

30/3/96

THANKS AND PRAISE offered to God shows true love.
    Glory and honour offered to God shows true humility.
    Worship and adoration offered to God shows true faith.

In faith find love and in love find humility.

1 CORINTHIANS 1:4
Never stop thanking God for all the graces you have received through Jesus Christ.

17/6/96

TO OFFER YOUR prayers for another is a wonderful gift to that person, a gift of love.
To offer the Mass for another is the greatest gift you can offer. With the Mass you offer My sacrifice for their forgiveness and you offer My body and blood in their name to the Father.

This offering is the greatest gift to give; a gift that can save a soul.

4/1/97

MY LOVE,
    My heart,
    My life,

All offered to mankind because I love them.

PSALMS 147:2 | *Yahweh, restorer of Jerusalem.*

9/1/97

WHEN YOU LOVE Me you must try to love everyone.
When you follow Me you must try to follow My example.
When you offer yourself to Me you must offer yourself to all as an example of what it means to love Me.

9/3/97

TO MAKE AN offer of love which is then rejected should not stop you offering more love.

3/5/97

MAKE EACH MOMENT count by offering it to Me in love.

7/5/97

EACH BREATH YOU take is a gift I give to you.
In love return each breath as a gift to Me.

PSALMS 21:4 | *He asked for life and you gave it him.*

Idolatry

14/12/96

IDOLATRY COMES IN many forms. It may be of other so-called gods which are often only deceptions to take people from the one true God, the Holy Trinity. It may be money, power, fame, self, other people who seem larger than life, or it may even be an acceptance of evil as the way to live. Idolatry is a sin and yet so many do not see this.

Often it is asked how worshipping a sport, a person who is successful or powerful can be a sin? Well, it becomes a sin when you ignore God and replace God in your life with these human things. It becomes a sin when these become the main reason for living. It becomes a sin when you hurt others by ignoring them in your worship of these things.

Idolatry comes in many forms and each one is only a way to take you from God and to hurt you and hurt others. Idolatry is accepted by many because they do not see what it truly is and often many educate their family and friends to accept this as part of life.

Mankind should remember only God should be worshipped. To worship anyone or anything no matter who or what they are is a sin, a sin that is often hidden.

JEREMIAH 39:22 | *They have misled you.*

Addictions

27/4/96

DRUGS ARE SENT from the cold heart of the evil one to trap My weak children. At first they bring joy and excitement then they bring hunger and no shame in what you do. Hunger for more drugs and a willingness to do anything to get them, seeing no shame in your actions.
How Satan laughs as sweet souls become sour, as healthy hearts become broken. Like all that is evil it hurts those who are close, so many families destroyed, so many lives taken, so many blind and foolish children.

JEREMIAH 51:34
He has devoured, consumed me, that king of Babylon: He has left me like an empty dish.

27/4/96

BROKEN HEARTS OF mothers around the world mourn for their children addicted to evil. Mothers who only love and want the best for their children cry tears of love as they see their children destroy themselves. A day comes when these mothers will have their prayers answered and their children saved.

ECCLESIASTICUS 23:27–37
And those who survive her will recognize that nothing is bet-
ter than fearing the Lord and nothing sweeter than adher-
ence to the Lord's commandments.

23/9/97

ONLY THE WEAK, the confused, the hurt, the lost, and the
selfish turn to drugs, for in drugs they find false strength,
false happiness, false security and false life which often leads to death, which often leads to destruction and
which always hurts the person and his family.

SIRACH 2:7 | *Turn not away lest you fall.*

Violence and War

3/1/96

TO ARM THE innocent makes them no longer innocent.

11/7/96

THE VIOLENCE BETWEEN men in the name of religion is a
violence sent to destroy religion and to destroy peace.
In the religious life that all should follow there is no room
for violence, only love.

25/8/97

TO KILL IS wrong, there is no excuse for it unless it is an acci-
dent. To kill is a sin and no reason changes this. To kill is
an affront to God and the love that God offers you.

Never kill no matter what.
Never kill no matter who justifies it.
Never kill no matter how you are persuaded to do so.

Killing another is wrong and it is a grave sin that can cost
your very soul.

ISAIAH 5:24
*For rejecting the Law of Yahweh Sabaoth, and despising the
word of the Holy One of Israel.*

Peace

19/12/95

PATIENCE BRINGS PEACE,
  Impatience brings anxiety.

7/1/96

AN ANGRY PERSON can find peace in Me.
  A lonely person can find comfort in Me.
  A lost person can find the way in Me.

14/2/96

IN SILENCE I am there.
  In peace find Me.
  In the quiet listen.

PSALMS 107:43
*If you are wise study these things and realize how Yahweh
shows his love.*

1/3/96

THE REMOVAL OF sin from the world will bring peace to
   mankind.
   To remove sin pray, trust and believe then see the darkness lifted and the light of My love shine brightly on all
   the world.

7/4/96

THE PEACE I offer is the peace that is found in My love.
   The love I offer is the love that brings peace.

14/3/97

BE AT PEACE in your heart,
       Be at peace in your life,
       Be at peace in My love.

   EZEKIEL 38:16 | *To display my holiness to them.*

2/7/97

CONFUSION REIGNS WHEN evil is near. Peace and tranquility
   reign where I am.

   EPHESIANS 3:8 | *The infinite treasure of Christ.*

3/12/97

BE AT PEACE in prayer.
   Be at peace in the Sacraments.

   Then be at peace in Me.

   TITUS 1:4
   Peace from God the Father and Christ Jesus our saviour.

Jerusalem

12/4/96

THERE WAS A man walking the road to Jerusalem. As He came close to the city He looked upon it and knew He loved it. He knew also Jerusalem would be the place of His death and the place where God's glory would be shown to the world.
I am that man and I am the Glory of God. Today I look upon Jerusalem and still love it.
Today Jerusalem is no different from when I walked the earth, so holy and yet so full of sin.

God's Will

29/3/96

TO DO MY will means to forget your demands and to surrender completely to Me. When you do this you find your needs fulfilled.

To do My wishes means to forget your demands and to surrender completely to Me. When you do this you find your needs fulfilled.

26/8/97

THE JUST WILL receive justice.
The honest will receive the truth.
The faithful will receive eternity.

Be faithful in doing My will and show justice to all by speaking My truth in complete honesty and you will find eternity awaiting.

PSALMS 52:10 | *Trust in God's faithful love forever.*

Justice

1/7/96

AS A JUST man receives justice so does a false man receive justice. The justice is the same, it is only the payment that is different.

ECCLESIASTICUS 11:5
Many monarchs have been made to sit on the ground and the man nobody thought of has worn the crown.

27/7/96

JUSTICE IS DONE when the truth wins.

Law

3/7/96

THE LAWS OF mankind must be adhered to when they are in agreement with God's law. Any man-made law that opposes God's law cannot be accepted and should be opposed by all those who love God, for what is your love of God if you accept that which offends Him.

27/1/97

TO ABIDE BY the law is the way you must live. The law of God first, then the law of man, only if it does not conflict with God's laws.

SONG OF SONGS 8:6 | *Set me like a seal on your heart.*

Technology

24/3/96

MAN'S MACHINES SHOULD be for the advancement of mankind, advancement in love, for without love how can you advance.

Doctors

8/7/96

A DOCTOR'S ROLE IS to save lives.
A doctor is gifted to save lives.
A doctor is graced to save lives.

Life is so valuable to Me that I give many gifts and graces to those in medicine so that the lives of My children can be helped and improved; not destroyed.

Judgement Day

Before God all men answer
for their actions.
How sad it is that many forget this.

ECCLESIASTICUS 12:5
Then you would be repaid evil.

The Reign of God

IN THE BEGINNING love reigned supreme.
In the end love will reign supreme.

Now is the time to discover love so that in the end you
can be part of that reign.

HOSEA 10:10 | *They will follow behind Yahweh.*

Books available from:

USA

Alan Ames Ministry
PO Box 200
233 Glasgow Avenue SW
Kellogg
Minnesota 55945

Phone: 507 767 3027
Web: http://www.alanames.org

Australia

Touch of Heaven
(Alan Ames Ministry)
PO Box 85
Wembley, 6014
West Australia

Phone: 61 89275 6608
Fax: 61 89382 4392
Web: http://www.alanames.ws
Email: touchofheaven@iinet.net.au